30 BIRDS
THAT WILL BUILD
IN BIRD HOUSES

R. B. LAYTON

NATURE
BOOKS
PUBLISHERS

NB

First Printing   1977

Mailing address:
NATURE BOOKS PUBLISHERS
Post Office Box 12157
Jackson, Mississippi 39211

Library of Congress Catalogue
Card Number: 77-81805.

International Standard Book
Number 0—912542—01—5

Printed in the United States of America

TO-

those who would care enough to assist nature in maintaining the life cycle of our avian friends ...

thus to enjoy even more that which is already about us from day to day

PREFACE

This book has been written for the purpose of encouraging nature lovers to attract birds to their home site, whether in the city, town, village or countryside. Its intentions are to provide pertinent information about each of thirty birds known to build in man-made houses, to provide many house designs to select from, to give specific directions for building each house, as well as to mention ways that one might attract these birds.

Although the author has included thirty birds that have been identified as house dwellers this does not mean that each of these will live on your premises, nor does it mean that these are the only birds that will build in bird houses. It does mean that among this thirty surely one can find a favorite and erect a house to provide the enjoyment of observing nature's progress in the growth cycle of our avian population.

The author has included the findings of others along with his own lifetime of observation. Books of general scope, included by the author in the select bibliography, were frequently consulted, particularly the series of author Cleveland Bent, **Life Histories of North American Birds**, originally published in 1921 by the Smithsonian Institution of Washington, D.C.

He wishes to extend his thanks to the following persons and organizations that have assisted in various ways in the preparation of this book: Bill Turcott and B. E. Gandy of the Mississippi Game and Fish Commission and State Wildlife Museum, David Allen and the Laboratory of Ornithology of Cornell University, Robert Pendleton, Dana Yensen, Hubert Prescott, Bitty Sneed, the Smithsonian Institution, and Dover Publications.

He wishes particularly to express a debt of gratitude to his wife, Gray Layton, without whose advice and assistance this volume might not have ever been.

R.B.L.

COVER PHOTO - WESTERN BLUEBIRD - BY HUBERT W. PRESCOTT

TABLE OF CONTENTS

INTRODUCTION

INTRODUCTION

HOW TO USE THIS BOOK

There are certain observations one must note as he reads the bird biography section on each bird. First, he should note the accompanying summer range map for the species to see if that particular bird is a summer dweller in his area. Birds generally restrict their nesting territories to the long established habitats of that species. For example, the tufted titmouse is shown to nest in the eastern part of the United States. Persons living in the western parts need not try to build and erect a house for this titmouse. It should be pointed out, however, that persons living in a geographical area that borders the suggested nesting boundary may well try to attract the species shown. The boundaries shown on each map approximate the area and do not establish a clear-cut division between nesting areas and non-nesting areas. It is well to keep this in mind.

SONGRAPHS INCLUDED

Pioneers in visual reproductions of bird songs were Dr. Peter Paul Kellogg and Cornell University in their audiospectrograms or sonagrams, which through later years have been used in many scientific publications. More recently they have been produced in a very popular field guide, **Birds of North America,** by Robbins, Bruun, and Zim.

We have included a different graph in this book, our **songraphs,** which are microwave patterns of the call of each species. The songraph is meant to be an aid in identification by song, not to determine specific notes on the music scale. By following the songraph one can tell the sound patterns. The height of the graph pattern from the baseline represents the amplitude or volume. (The higher the line, the louder the sound). The width of the distance between the lines represents the frequency or pitch, of the sound. (The closer the lines the higher the pitch). The chart is read from left to right. The overall pattern represents the degree of stress when the sounds are uttered.

The audible modulations (am), or the sounds we hear, are the "up and down" lines which have a frequency range of roughly 200-450 cycles per second, about two to three times that of the human voice. The up and down pattern of the am frequency is the frequency modulation (fm) pattern, which is what we cannot hear. The restriction of this pattern represents the degree of stress present.

Let us look at the tree swallow songraph. The sounds

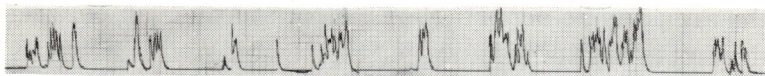

TREE SWALLOW

(chirps) were uttered at a frequency of approximately three times per second. (The length of each graph chart represents about two and one-half seconds). The tree swallow's wide range of amplitude shows a coarse voice similar to a human voice, where certain utterences of the Bob White show a narrow range of amplitude, representing a clearer, more refined sound.

2

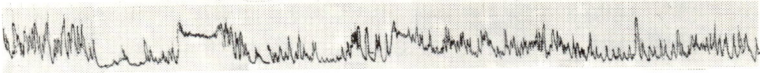

The wood duck call shown below has a distinctive pattern in that the graph does not return to the base line for an

WOOD DUCK

extended period of time. Its sound is continuous, varying in pitch but little in amplitude. There are small areas of heavy stress patterns evidenced in this chart indicating that this bird may have been under some sort of stress producing influence at the time the sound was recorded.

ACTUAL EGG SIZE SHOWN

4-8, 5-6 common;
white to buff
greyish brown
speckled

We have also shown (see left) the actual egg size for each bird along with a description and dimensions of each egg. In addition, there is an indication of the clutch range. We are including this egg information to assist the birder in identification of the bird, not to suggest collecting bird eggs, for indeed, private collections of wild birds eggs are now outlawed by the Federal Migration Bird Act — as they should be.

BIRD HOUSE PLANS

A very significant section of this book shows the bird houses that one can make or can have made. The large number and styles that the author has shown offer quite a variety from which the intended birder may choose. For materials the author suggests using exterior or marine grade plywood, one-fourth inch thick, cypress or western cedar boards of about one-half inch thickness, or bark slabs, sawed or split from log sections, as well as small cross-sections. Various modifications of your own choosing may be applied to these suggested plans.

Each bird house is shown as a simplified drawing with a narrative description of just how to build the house. At the end of each general house building narrative will be found the names of the birds that generally will use that particular house, since the same style and size or variations of size will attract several different species in many situations. The location of the house, its style, size, and diameter of the entrance hole are important determinants to be considered.

PURCHASING MATERIAL FOR
THE BIRD HOUSE

When purchasing plywood it is well to remember that one need not always buy an entire standard four foot by eight foot sheet. Lumber yards, hardware stores, and building material suppliers usually will cut a sheet in half (sometimes smaller). Use the yellow pages and make inquiry by phone before you go.

Cypress end pieces, from one to two feet in length and six to ten inches in width can be bought at the fence dealers. These ends are about one-half inch thick and are scrap material cut from ends of fence boards, usually priced economically. Sometimes redwood and western cedar can be found in short lengths also. These boards are usually rough, unplaned, but make a beautiful bird house when permitted to weather with time. Do not paint these boards if you wish them to weather attractively. These materials suggested are all of long-lasting quality, which is important.

In constructing the house we suggest using an aluminum nail to prevent rusting, a one and one-fourth inch "cedar shingle" type, usually bought in a box from the hardware store. If aluminum nails are not available, a small finishing nail or casing nail may also be used. Be sure that these non-aluminum nails are coated with some non-corrosive substance to prevent their rusting.

Your bird house should always have one-fourth inch diameter ventilation holes drilled through the sides at a position near the top of each floor or room. There should also be similar holes drilled through the floor to let rain water drain out that might blow into the room through the door, or otherwise. Especially are these drain holes of great importance when using gourds, since they tend to collect water in the bottom cupped areas.

Remember that bird houses, if painted, should be of light colored paint, white preferably, to reflect the extreme heat, if erected in the sunlight. Otherwise, when painting try to match the environment.

A trip to a nearby lumber mill will produce excellent bark-on scrap slab pieces to use in birdhouse construction ( ). These can be found in random lengths, which offer a wide choice and are usually inexpensive or free. If procuring whole small log cross-sections presents a difficulty, try firewood dealers from your newspaper want-adds. These will suggest a place that you might procure your cross-section pieces.

PURCHASING A HOUSE
INSTEAD OF BUILDING ONE

We realize that not all people are builders and some will prefer to purchase their bird houses. In order to care for this we recommend that you visit your nearby hardware store, seed and feed store, or yard and garden supplier. These stores usually carry bird houses for sale. A word of caution here, be sure that the house you purchase is of such design and size that the bird you wish to attract will use it. Some bird houses on the market will not attract any bird, except perhaps the house sparrow or starling. In the appendix we have listed several reputable national dealers from whom you can purchase bird houses.

SILHOUETTES

With each species the author has shown a silhouette of that species in comparison with a silhouette of the mockingbird, the latter selected because of its generally known size, wide range across the entire country, and the common knowledge of its appearance to practically everyone. Here is an example of the silhouette that is shown in the titmouse section in comparison with the mockingbird.

NOMENCLATURE

Obviously a woodpecker is so named because it pecks on wood, a flycatcher because it catches flies, but why is a martin called a martin? a titmouse called a titmouse? a finch called a finch? a starling called a starling? and so on.

For those birds among our thirty not obviously named, we have sought out the derivation of their names, known to ornithologists and in ornithological literature but not commonly known to those of us claiming to be only naturalists, and we have given a brief introductory treatment to their origin purely for interest sake.

BIRD PHOTOGRAPHS

While this book is not meant to be a bird guide in the strickest sense we have tried to make it usable for this if one chooses, since it goes far beyond the guide technique in furnishing information. We have sought out the very finest photographs by leading naturalists and ornithologists to assist the birder in identifying each bird. Many of these photographs have never been published.

SELECTED BIBLIOGRAPHY INCLUDED

The partial bibliography included contains valuable reference books for further reading for those desiring to add to their library. In no way is this list meant to be all inclusive, but it does contain valuable birding information recommended by the author. He has annotated each to assist the reader in making a selection.

FEEDING BIRDS

Planting of berry, fruit, and seed-producing vegetation for the birds is a proven way of attracting them to your home site. Winter feeding with supplementary bought seeds is also rewarding.

Some birders feed the year round. This is an admirable

trait but not as essential as is the winter feeding. We should point out here that once winter feeding has begun it should be continued — for birds soon become dependent upon your feeding station, often for their survival during an icy, snowy, or sub-freezing period.

There are many feeders on the market, all of which may be used by the birds; but there are particular types of feeders for particular species of birds. Where you feed is important, too, for some birds eat from the ground, some from a low feeder, some from a high feeder, and so on.

The common type of mixed feed usually found at the grocery market is a good all-purpose feed to use. Sunflower seeds, both shelled and unshelled, are favorites of most birds, particularly of the grosbeaks, finches, titmice, chickadees, thrashers, mocking birds and cardinals. Goldfinches and purple finches will readily choose your Ethiopian Niger (thistle) seed, but a special cylindrical single seed dispenser is best for this, saving seeds, and preventing other birds from using it. Sparrows, starlings, and squirrels do not seem to care for this seed, a recommendation for its use. A flower pot saucer attached to the bottom of the cylinder by a simple macrame designed cord will catch the fallen seeds and provide yet another favorite eating place for these birds. Instead, you may purchase a metal base for this.

Suet feeders are easily made and suet (animal fat) is easily found at most any super market at little or no cost. The suet may be attached to the side of a tree, hung from a tree limb in a knit bag, secured behind hardware cloth of various sizes and patterns, or attached on the side of a feeder.

One of the most desired feeders is a homemade mixed peanut butter and seed feeder. This feeder can be made by taking a section of tree limb from a small tree of about two to three inches in diameter and drilling one-inch holes about an inch deep or more, being sure not to bore through the section. These holes can be bored at random around the sides of the tree section. A section of two inch by two inch board may be substituted for the tree or limb section but is not as handsome or rustic as the tree or limb section.

The squirrel often frequents the feeders, causing concern to the provider. We suggest that you consolidate most of your feeders on one pole. A cluster of these can be arranged into an attractive presentation (see drawing that follows). Then, to prevent a squirrel's taking over, attach a square or round baffle of clear plactic sheet or metal on the pole at a height of seven or eight feet, being certain that the feeders are above this height. Another type of squirrel guard is made by using a sliding section of light weight aluminum pipe or plastic pipe over the pole as a part of a pulley system (see drawing) with a weight inside that is slightly heavier than that of the sliding section in order to keep the section at the top always, near the pulley wheel. As the squirrel climbs the pipe and attempts to climb across the sliding section of pipe, his weight makes the section of pipe slide down with him aboard. As the pipe section reaches the bottom, or before, and the squirrel leaps off, the section will then rise back to the pulley height. Since the squirrel is of such light weight, it is important to use a.very light weight section of pipe, such as aluminum, otherwise, the squirrel may complete his climb across the section before it moves downward.

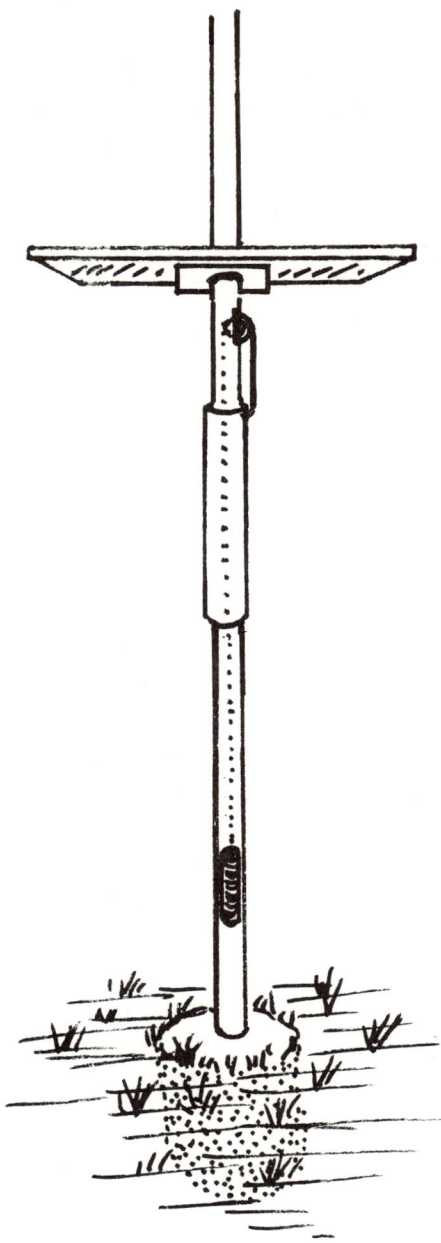

PROVIDING VEGETATION FOR THE BIRDS

For those wishing to attract birds to their premises the following fruit-bearing vegetation is suggested:

American Holly
Arrowwood
Aster
Bachelors Button
Bayberry
Birch
Blackberry
Black Haw
Blueberry
Cherry
Columbine
Coreopsis
Crab Apple
Cranberry
Deciduous Holly
Dogwood
Elderberry
Fennel
Forget-me-not
Greenbrier
Ground Juniper
Hackberry
Hawthorne
Hemlock
Honeysuckle
Inkberry
Maple
Mountain Ash
Mulberry
Muscadine

Nannyberry
Oak Acorn
Oregon Grape Holly
Persimmon
Phlox
Photinia
Plantain
Plum
Poppy
Pyracantha
Raspberry
Red Cedar
Sassafras
Scuppernong
Shadbush
Snowberry
Sunflower
Spicebush
Sour Gum
Spruce
Sycamore
Tulip Tree
Virginia Creeper
Winterberry
Willow
Yaupon
Zinnia

Providing seed, berry, and fruit vegetation can assist appreciably in attracting birds to your premises. We suggest that you plant some of these that we have mentioned. Select ones that will grow in your geographical area.

PROVIDING NEST
BUILDING MATERIALS

You can assist the birds with their nest building by providing string for them to use in their nest building. Various kinds and colors of string may be used. The string should be cut into lengths of six or eight inches to prevent tangles as well as to make it easy for the birds to remove. The string should be placed in some type of container such as a tomato or berry basket, a small can, or a wire cup made of hardware cloth or screen wire and attached to a tree or to a fence post.

The fluffy lint from the automatic clothes dryer trap will readily be accepted by birds also. We suggest that a second container be used for this, however. Do not mix it with the string. Use your imagination and memory in providing various types of nesting materials. A start could be pine straw, very short twigs, hay cuttings, Spanish moss, and other materials.

A HELP IN PREVENTING
WASP TAKEOVER

Since wasps and bees like to build nests on hard surfaces and in dry places, they often will build their nests in your bird houses. Some bird enthusiasts have found that by putting a thin layer of cup grease or vaseline on the ceiling and sides of the bird house the wasps and bees will not build. You might try this if wasps and bees present a problem.

CONTROLING OTHER
INSECT INFESTATION

There are several ways in which the infestation of other insects can be controlled, particularly the mites and lice that so often cause the birds to leave the nest and the young to die.

Sevin dust, sulphur dust, or environmentally approved insecticides may be used to control insects. None of these mentioned will contaminate the apartments or the houses to hurt the birds. When cleaning out the house each year, dust the interior with one of the safe insecticides. To make sevin dust last for a longer time, mix it with water in a ratio of two tablespoonsful per ounce of water. Keep it stirred while painting the inside of the bird house or gourd. The water will soak into the wood or evaporate from the gourd, wood, or metal siding and leave a fine coating of the sevin powder that will cling to the walls and be effective for a much longer period of time.

DISCOURAGING THE SPARROWS
AND STARLINGS

Some have found that cedar shavings and cedar bough clippings dusted with the sulphur dust and placed inside the bird house or apartment will discourage sparrows and starlings from building. About a half cup of the combined mixtures should be placed inside of each area. The boughs should be cut with the scissors or snips into one-half inch to one inch pieces. Fresh, newly cut boughs and shavings should be used to gain the greatest aroma, of course. While this primarily is recommended for purple martin houses, since the martins find the aroma to be acceptable, it also may prove to be acceptable to the species that you are trying to attract. Our experience with this does not permit us to recommend this for every bird house. One should experiment with this first in sparrow infested boxes to determine whether the intended birds will accept this mixture after the sparrow or starling nests have been removed and the mixture placed therein. Even if the mixture does not discourage the sparrow or starling, it will prove to be helpful in controlling the mites and lice.

BIOGRAPHIES

1

CAROLINA WREN
(Thrýóthorus ludoviciánus)
length - 5½ to 6½ inches

There are ten species of wrens that are native to North America. Among the ten, however, there are only three that are generally known to be attracted to houses, the Carolina wren, the house wren, and the Bewick's wren.

The Carolina wren is brownish red above with a grayish white hue below. Just above the eye it has a white streak that runs from the forehead to the back of the head. The tail and wings are barred with a dusky brown. The feet and legs are dark flesh colored and the bill is dark gray.

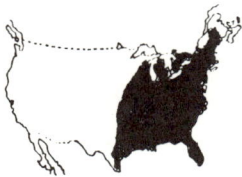

The little Carolina wren is a summer dweller in practically all of the eastern half of the United States. Its nesting area now reaches as far northeast as Maine and west to Minnesota and Oklahoma. It is easily identified at a glance by its cocky tail, usually in a vertical position, by its white eyestripe, and by its distinctive song that can be heard in all kinds of weather. At nest building time it searches out its own preferred nesting site, which may be a tree fork, a tree cavity, shelf, bird house, or some very unorthodox place.

The wren gets its name from Middle English "wrenne", Anglo-Saxon and Old English "wrenna" and akin to Old

High German "rentilo" and Old Norse "rendill" — all meaning "small singing bird."

My own experience with the Carolina wren is that it selects a most unusual place to nest, one that you would never suggest, nor offer. At the beginning of the spring season I had hung my new navy blue swim trunks on a clothes rack attached to the back of the house-where we usually dried our swim wear after a dip in the lake behind the house. A couple of days later when reaching for these trunks I noticed a Carolina wren flying out. Upon closer examination, I discovered an almost completed nest inside. Question — turn over my new swim trunks to a bird, or carefully remove the partial nest and place it in the old (red) trunks to be placed in the same location. Deciding upon the latter, with the utmost care I removed the nest from the new blue trunks and placed it in the red ones and then carefully placed them in the same position on the rack. I then waited to see what would happen. Very soon, in fact almost immediately, the little wren came back looked the red trunks over carefully, went inside the garment, came out, and flew away. I stayed long enough to see if he would return. He did, and without any lost time, carrying a twig of grass to continue the nest building. This pair raised three young wrens in this further undisturbed domicile that season.

On another occasion, my wife decided to water a high hanging basket of ferns on the patio and when she did, out flew a Carolina wren. It did not nest there but roosted there every night with its mate during the fall and into the winter.

An old hat, a tin can, an apron, almost anything that one

hangs on the wall seems to be more desirable than a house sometimes. Regardless, though, whether man made house or otherwise, having a wren family through the nesting or roosting season is a delight to observe.

The art instructor at a private high school invited me into the art department, when I was there on a school evaluation program, to see a wren nest with a wren thereon, made in one of the pockets of her smock that was hanging on an art easel. The wren had come through a window that was left ajar and the instructor, being a bird lover, gave up the smock for the season, left the window ajar each day and went right ahead with her class of art students. This added a new interest to the group and seemed not to disturb the wrens, for they eventually raised their brood and departed.

When no human dwelling appeals, the Carolina wren's wooded resorts may be an undergrowth near water, in a fallen tree top, in a brush heap, rocky places in the woods, or some similar places.

This wren is indeed the symbol of restless energy, bobbing up and down and assuming various poses and is so domestic that he is often referred to as "house wren", meaning a bird around the house, to distinguish it from the regular house wren. In fact, as I now write, within six feet of my desk, and outside on the deck of our second floor balcony, I can see through the picture window this little wren giving me a "once over" look, perhaps seeking a wintering place to roost, for it is the middle of December now. Its whistled song of "teakettle, teakettle, teakettle" is a delight to hear.

5 common; whitish, spotted with brown. .74 in. x .60 in.

If you decide to build a lodging place for this capricious little creature, your wren house could be placed near your own dwelling and at a height of six to eight feet, with an entrance hole one inch in diameter. Try to choose a place under the eaves or against the side of the house, or on top of a cabinet, on a sheltered porch, but don't be surprised if he selects a place in an old flower pot, watering can hanging on the wall, hat, hole in the wall, pail, basket, empty box, or otherwise. Accept him, though, wherever he builds, for he will entertain you for a long time.

The Carolina wren uses for its nest sticks, dry grasses, dry leaves, weed stalks, lining the nest with feathers and hair. The nest varies in size, depending upon the volume of the area chosen. Sometimes the nest is very large but usually is compact and so skillfully made that it can easily be lifted intact. This wren is a meticulous nest builder.

The period of incubation is 12 to 14 days, and the young remain in the nest about the same length of time. The female usually performs the brooding task but both parents tend to the feeding. The pair usually stay mated, returning year after year to the same nest or box.

Observations of the stomach contents by ornithologists have shown that its food is about 95% animal matter, nearly all insects. The rest is vegetable matter, mainly seeds. The insects are almost entirely the injurious type. The wren's insect food included: weevils, beetles, leafhoppers, chinch bugs, caterpillars, moths, crickets, roaches, daddylonglegs, crane flies, sowbugs and snails. The seeds included: bayberries, sweet gum, poison ivy, sumac, pine, acorns, and various weed seeds.

This bird will come to the feeding stations, particularly for the peanut butter and seed mixture and can fend for himself against any contender, regardless of size.

The Carolina wren is often referred to as "Jenny Wren" or "Johnny Wren."

The wren, in general, has been referred to as "bobby,"

"cutty", "sally", "scutty", "tiddy", "titty", "Our Lady of Heaven", (English folklore), "great Carolina wren," "Mocking wren".

It raises one brood only each year.

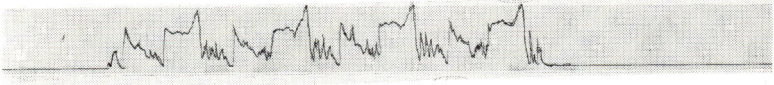

PHOTO BY ARTHUR A. ALLEN, CORNELL UNIV.

CAROLINA WREN

2.

BEWICK'S WREN
(Thryómanes béwickii)
length - 5½ inches

The Bewick's (pronounced Buick's) wren was named by John James Audubon for his friend Thomas Bewick, famous English engraver. It, like other wrens, will be found nesting in a variety of places.

Its range basically is across the middle United States. Its nesting territory is usually where the house wren is not found to nest for the two do not get along together well, always competing, and the Bewick's wren is no match for the more aggressive house wren. It becomes the "house wren" for its area. It will seldom be found nesting in the southern half of the United States.

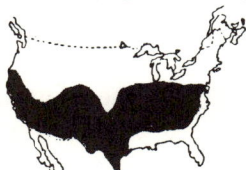

Very similar to the Carolina wren in its habits, it will be found nesting in knotholes of fallen trees, woodpecker holes, bush heaps, holes in fence posts, barrels, old hats, clothing left hanging outside of the house, baskets, crevices in stone walls, or elsewhere. Cited by some naturalists as preferring to be in the barn than about man's house, it still locates itself near members of the human family whenever the site suits his taste.

Distinguished from other wrens by its tail wobbling from side to side, its tail feathers are black barred and white tipped, a mark not found on other wrens. It, too, has a white eyeline like the Carolina wren and unless the two are seen together you are not likely to distinguish between the two by the eye line. This wren has white to smoky gray under parts with a dusky brown top and side markings. It is slightly smaller than the Carolina wren, but slightly larger than the house wren. It is common and widespread in the southwest but uncommon in the Appalachian region.

The Bewick's wren is a very fine singer with "sweet and tender strains throughout its song." When it is alarmed, a single or double "plit" can be heard for a quarter-mile or more. Its melodious song, a "chip-chip-tee-da-tee-de", causes it to be often called the "Mockingbird wren," or "mocking wren."

The house of the Bewick wren should be placed from six to ten feet off the ground and somewhere about the house, garage, or barn. The entrance hole should be one inch in diameter to keep out larger birds. Observe the wren habits when it visits and then select an area that it seems to like, against the wall, under an eave, on a shelf, hanging flower pot, or other likely place.

This wren builds its nest of sticks, straw, feathers, chips, moss, dead leaves, cotton, hair, and occasionally a piece of plastic bag or snake skin. It lines its nest with soft feathers and may use the lint from your clothes drier, if provided.

The period of incubation is ten to fourteen days with the young remaining another fourteen days. The young are fed by both parents but the female does the incubating.

Its food consists of: boll weevils, green worms, moths, caterpillars, beetles, and other small insects. A very minor portion of its diet is vegetable matter, weed seeds particularly. It eats very much the same diet that the other wrens eat.

5-7, 7 common; white, spotted with reddish brown .6 in. x .5 in.

The Bewick's wren is also often referred to as "Jenny Wren" or "Johnny Wren," like its Carolina wren cousin, and a "long tailed house wren". It raises one brood a year.

BEWICK'S WREN

3

HOUSE WREN
(Troglódytes aédon)
length - 4½ to 5¼ inches

This is by far the most common wren to use bird houses.

The house wren nests across southern Canada and the upper two thirds of the United States. It competes with the Bewick's wren where the two nesting areas coincide, usually getting the best of the encounter. It, too, is very lively and a nervous bundle of energy. The house wren is buffy brown above and smoky-gray below with flesh colored legs and dark brown eyes. It has darker brown barring on its wings and tail. The bill of the house wren is basically yellow but with a brownish-black tip. Its tail, too, is cocked up at an angle.

The male usually appears first to locate a nesting site and stake out the territory. He is likely to choose most any old thing cast off by man, such as a tin can, basket, barrel, old hat, garbage pail, cavity in a brick wall, or knot hole in the side of the house. The male starts the nest using the most likely material at hand, including twigs, grass, moss, feathers, and other nearby things. As soon as the female appears courtship begins, with the male singing to attract her attention. When nest building begins and she decides to take over, she is likely to discard the male's feeble attempt at nest building and begin anew, using strange cast offs of people, such as hairpins, nails, staples, paper clips, beer can popouts, buckles, or other items - of course, along with twigs, grass, moss, feathers and the like. Do not try to provide items for the wren to use for it prefers to choose its own.

The house wren will usually accept the Carolina wren in its area but for some reason it very much dislikes the Bewick's wren, driving it away whenever it appears.

The house wren seems to prefer areas of low woody vegetation, deciduous and brushy. The edges of a wooden area, with sunny openings within the forest are selected very often.

It carries no particular markings to make it distinct. Perhaps, though, its gray-brown color is enough, since the absence of eyelines, white markings and other characteristics single it out as the house wren.

Occasionally the house wren will go into other bird nests or houses, puncture the eggs or kill the young. It will often attack the larger birds if furious scolding will not drive them away.

The male is known to build a second nest nearby, either to offer more attraction to his mate or to attract another female, which he does at times.

Often this wren will nest in an apartment of a Purple Martin house and raise a brood there. They have been known to take over nests of other birds on occasions also.

Observation of nest building of the house wren and other wrens also, will prove quite entertaining as this bird struggles to get unwieldy sticks through the small one inch entrance hole. It may seek entry with its beak grasped at the center of a long twig, finding out from trial and error that there must be a better way, and finally reaching accomplishment.

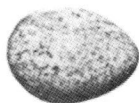

5-10
dull white,
densely spotted
with brown
.7 in. x .5 in.

The wren's house should be placed from six to eight feet above the ground or floor, on the side of a tree, wall of the house, swinging from a wire, or similar locations as for other wrens.

The incubation period of the house wren is thirteen to fifteen days, depending upon temperature, which is always an important factor in speeding up or delaying the usual incubation time. The time spent by the newly hatched wrens in the nest is from twelve to eighteen days. The brood is fed by both male and female. During the incubation period the female is fed by the male while she is on the nest. Only one brood is raised each year.

Usually the adults stay with the young for most of the twelve to eighteen days but for the last two or three days they expect the young to find their own food - which they do. As the young establish the ability to forage for themselves the adults spend less time with them, finally breaking away entirely. It is then that each individual is on its own.

The house wren's food also consists almost entirely of insects that are destructive to crops which makes the house wren welcomed by farmers and city gardeners. The small amount of vegetable matter eaten is thought to be purely incidental, usually plucked as it catches its insects. Its diet consists of grasshoppers, beetles, caterpillars, spiders, stink bugs, leafhoppers, crickets, locusts, ants, wasps, flies, sow bugs, millipedes, ticks, lice, aphids, snails, May beetles, moths, and other insects. While it devours some insects that are not harmful to crops, its main diet is those that are harmful and it thereby becomes one of our favored bird friends.

This wren, too, is likely to be dubbed "Johnny Wren" or "Jenny Wren". Also, some refer to it as the "wood" wren.

While not a common name, it is interesting to note that long ago the Chippewa Indians recognized its loud, clear, melodious song, a series of short bursts in rapid rise and fall repeats, by referring to it as "Odunamissugudla-weshi", meaning "a big noise for its size".

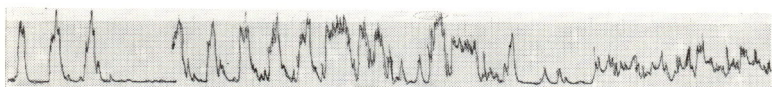

HOUSE WREN

4.

CAROLINA CHICKADEE
(Párus carolinénsis)
length - 5¾ inches

This little bird is perhaps our tamest visitor to the bird feeders. He will quickly come to your suet feeder, sunflower seed feeder, your mixed bird feeder, or any other, and will scold you severely if you permit his seed to run out.

The Carolina chickadee was named by Audubon from birds that were taken near Charleston, South Carolina. It sings a melodious "chicks dee-dee-dee-dee..." song throughout the southern states. The chickadee gets its name from the note it sounds.

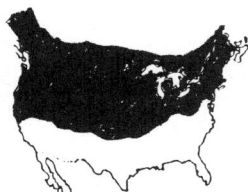

The blackcapped chickadee, frequenting our northern states and southern Canada is very similar to the Carolina chickadee, slightly larger, but distinguished from the Carolina chickadee better by locality than by appearance.

Both of these species will build in a man made bird house with one inch diameter entrance size and need little encouragement to become year-round residents. They flock together in winter, roaming the woodlands for insects and eating from man-provided feeders. The chickadee is easily distinguished from other small birds by its white cheeks and black cap with fringed black bib below. It has flanks of gray but they are whiter on the under side. The bill, legs, and feet are black, and it has a long tail. These little birds may come to your feeder alone or in pairs, the latter more frequently.

Since the chickadee uses vacant woodpecker holes, tree cavities, holes in fence posts, decayed stumps, open iron pipes of clothes lines, bridge supports, and many other available nitches, your best luck will be in placing the house near this type of locality. Its height above the ground should be from six to twelve feet and the house should be small in size. It is utterly amazing in how small a space this creature can build a nest.

The chickadee makes its nest of green moss, strips of bark, some grass, thistle down or milkweed pod down and feathers. Occasionally, animal fur, such as rabbit or squirrel fur will be found lining the nest. While the female has been found to do most of the nest construction, the male does assist - particularly if the two are excavating an old deserted hole or rotten cavity for a nest. About two weeks usually are needed for the two to complete their nesting cavity, depending upon the softness of the wood. When a cavity is excavated, the dimensions are minimal, two to six inches only, and, again, depending upon the wood being cut into.

Both sexes take turns in incubating the eggs. This lasts for about twelve days and the young remain in the nest for about fourteen to eighteen more days before the first flight takes place.

The food of the chickadee consists of about 75% animal matter and 25% vegetable matter. Moths and caterpillars are its favorite food, but bugs such as leafhoppers, stink bugs, treehoppers, plant lice, scales, ants, bees, wasps, beetles, cockroaches, katydids, and spiders are also consumed.

5-8, 6 common; white, finely brown spotted

Among its vegetable matter favorites will be found blackberries, blueberries and poison ivy seeds.

This little versatile bird is adept at procuring its food from trunk and bough, tip of the tree to the ground, not missing a crack or cranny where insect eggs and insects hide. No bug is too small to be overlooked as this acrobat performs his food gathering. Its insect eradication value is high, making it a welcomed visitor both in winter and in summer.

It is often referred to as "black cap", "black-capped titmouse", or just "dee-dee".

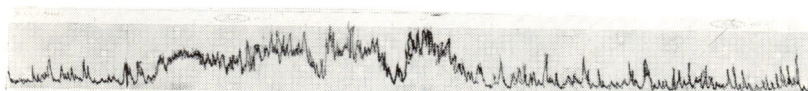

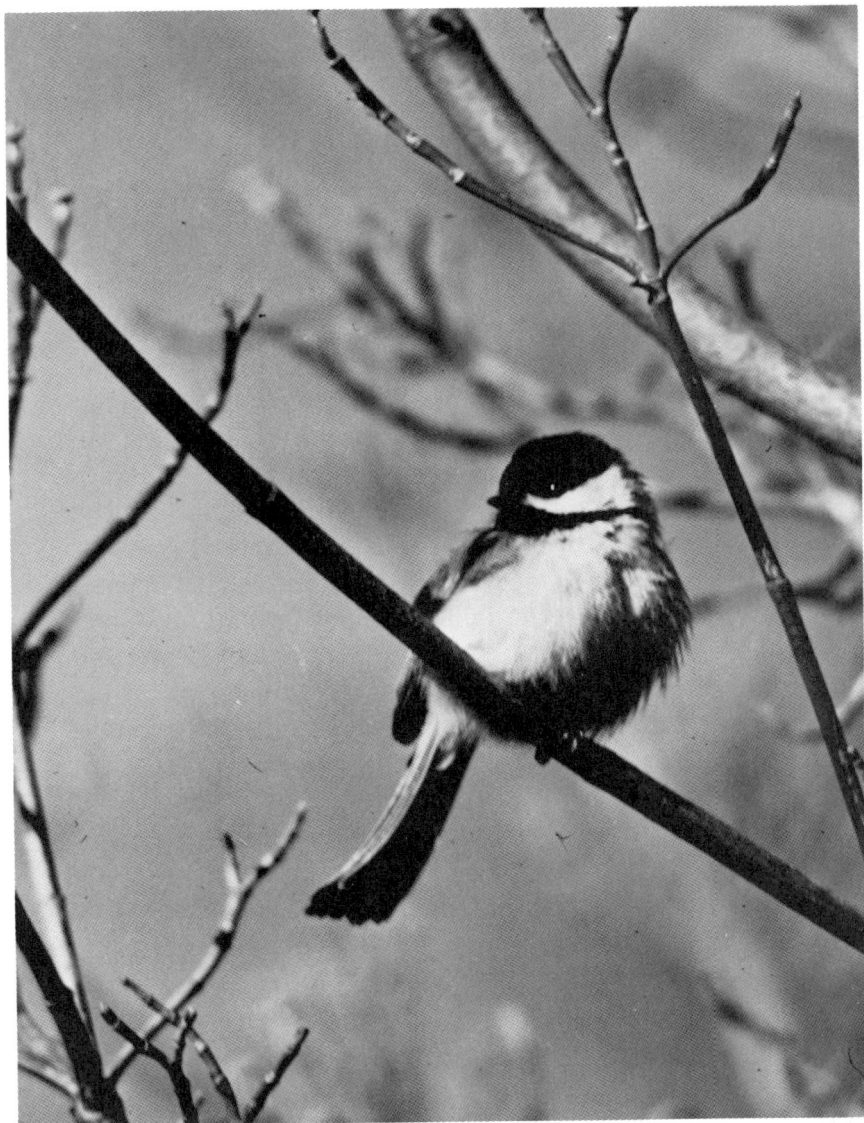

PHOTO BY DAVID G. ALLEN

BLACK-CAPPED CHICKADEE

5.

TUFTED TITMOUSE
(Párus bícolor)
length - 5½ to 6½ inches

The titmouse gets its name from **tit** meaning small and **mosé** (Anglo-Saxon) meaning small bird. In Medieval English it was called **titemosé**. The **mosé** form was later corrupted to **mouse** for its smallness and quick mouse-like movements.

A favorite throughout eastern United States this delightful little bird is easily attracted to winter feeders and to summer bird houses. Its delightful loud, whistling "peto, peto", or "peter, peter", repeated from three to eleven times is sometimes mistaken for the Carolina wren and can be heard across woods and meadow throughout the year. Not known to be shy in any respect, it darts fearlessly to the feeder, leaving no doubt that it means to get its tasty morsel, regardless of who else is at the feeder.

A favorite pastime of the feed provider is to observe this little bird take a sunflower seed to a nearby limb, hold it against the limb with its toes, whack it open, eat its kernel and then fly back to the feeder for a repeat performance.

The titmouse can be recognized as a small gray bird with a blackish tuft, chestnut brown flanks, smaller in size than an English sparrow, but larger than the chickadee. Its feet and legs are gray-black and its tail is gray. With black bill, it has a patch of gray between the bill and its brown eyes. The female wears a duller color than the male, although a similarly designed plumage. No other small gray bird has a tufted crest.

It is often seen with the chickadee, roaming about from yard to yard during the winter and has no hesitancy in joining other birds at the feeders.

The tufted titmouse seems to prefer deciduous forests for its nesting place, building in almost any kind of tree where there is a cavity, hole, or discarded woodpecker hole. It has been found to nest in beech, white, red and live oaks, tupelos, sycamores, pines, hemlocks, apple trees, mulberry trees, maples, locusts, ashs, chestnuts, and other hardwoods.

It readily builds in bird houses placed at about any height, from five to one hundred feet and will continue to use the site from year to year. Be sure the house entrance hole is only about one and one-fourth inches in diameter. I would suggest placing the house on the side of a tree in which you have seen a titmouse flitting about and at a height easily reached by you on a step ladder, about ten to twelve feet above the ground.

I have had a titmouse build in my much larger flicker house and raise a brood, also in a wren house that was about ten feet off the ground. The deep house has the advantage of preventing a predator from disturbing the nest, eggs or the young. However, the small entrance hole usually suffices for this.

The nesting materials used by the titmouse include: strips of bark, dead oak leaves, green moss, grass, animal fur and hair, as well as bits of rags, strings, or cloth. It has been reported as being daring enough to pluck hair from a live squirrel tail, woodchuck's back, and even a human's head. This little scrapper is determined always and seemingly afraid of nothing.

4-8, 5-6 common; white to buff grayish brown speckled

Incubation is approximately twelve days with the young then remaining for fifteen to twenty days. Incubation and brooding is mainly by the female, if not entirely, while both sexes feed the young. One brood a year is raised.

Its food consists of about two-fifths animal matter and one-fifth vegetable matter. Insect food includes: caterpillars, wasps, beetles, boll weevils, bees, stink bugs, treehoppers, scales, flies, katydids, and cockroaches. Vegetable matter includes: raspberries, blackberries, strawberries, elderberries, hackberries, blueberries, huckleberries, mulberries, bayberries, wax myrtle, acorns, chinquapins, beechnuts, dogwood berries, Virginia creeper berries, Japanese honeysuckle berries, and the seeds of tulip tree pods.

The titmouse is frequently called "Topknot", "Tomtit", "Tit", "Peter bird", or just "Tom", in both oral and written references.

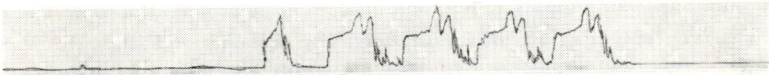

TUFTED TITMOUSE

6.

WHITE-BREASTED NUTHATCH
(Sítta carolinénsis)
length - 5 to 6¼ inches

The nuthatch gets its name from Middle English words **notehach, nuthake, nuttehoke,** and **nothak** (nut plus hack or hatch) from its characteristics of hacking on nuts or putting them away.

The white-breasted nuthatch frequents the entire United States and southern Canada. The species in different areas may vary in size and color, since some thirty are known to distribute themselves across the states. The white-breasted is the largest and most widespread, ranging in summer throughout the area shown on the map and is likely to be the one most seen in any territory.

The nuthatch is a fearless bird, commonly seen running up one side of a tree and down the other side. It seems to matter little whether he scampers with head up or head down going in an upside down position depending upon his claws for support, unlike the woodpecker that uses its tail for bracing itself.

It has a black cap, black naped neck, and beady black eyes on a white face. Its under parts are white and its top side is a mixture of blue and gray with some black on its wing and tail. There is a chestnut hue under the tail. The legs and feet are gray-black and its pointed black bill has a slight upward curve.

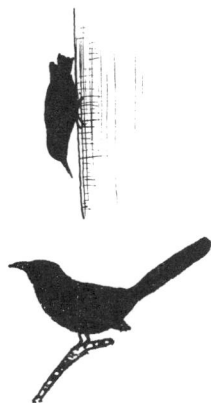

The nuthatch is a great musician, using low nasal calls and often sounding like a man whistling for his dog, becoming full, resonant, and mellow toward the end of its call. There is usually a regular series of six or eight notes, "yank, yank...", sharply accented, the same pitch, but each with a slightly rising inflection.

One of its characteristics is to pause in its upsidedown climb to extend its neck backward, the bill pointing straight outward at a ninety degree angle from the limb, as if to stretch its neck.

It will spend long hours at your bird feeder, going back and forth from feeder to tree or loose shingle on the house or barn, wedging its morsel securely in the crack, as if it would soon starve to death. A great deal of its time is spent in storing away food, much to the delight of the squirrels, jays, and other birds. Not deterred a bit as its food is taken, it continues to store food for another day. This nervous little bird, wedging its nuts or seeds into tree crevices, was well deserving of its name by the English who commonly called it "nuthack" and also by the French who referred to it as "notehatche", both because of its nut hiding characteristics.

Seeds and suet will bring the nuthatches to your feeders and rainy days do not deter their continued visitation.

Often mistaken for a woodpecker, the nuthatch's upsidedown run upon close observation will soon dispel this false identification.

It is a bird of the open pinewoods in southern United States but roams elsewhere for visiting and feeding and sometimes for mating.

As spring approaches, the male's attraction to his mate approaches also and he begins a real courtship, whereas in winter he may pay her little or no attention, often showing both rudeness and dominance over her at the feeding station. During mating time, however, he displays unusual attention to her. He will even carry food to her and place it in her mouth, storing bits of food nearby for her ready usage. During this time he will sing to her, strut before her, and give her his undivided attention. This is a most entertaining sight.

5-10
white, speckled
or spotted with
brown
.8 in. x .6 in.

While the nuthatch may often prefer a tree hole, cavity, or discarded woodpecker hole, it will also nest in a man-made bird box willingly-particularly if it resembles a tree section.

The nuthatch has been observed to be a very tame bird, showing little suspicion toward human beings. In fact, with a little patience, this bird can be induced to feed from your hand, some have said, particularly if one feeds from indoors through a crack in the window over the feeding shelf from which it has been feeding regularly.

Better luck will be had with the nuthatch house location where large oaks are found, particularly if some are decayed. Houses with a one and one-fourth inch diameter entrance that are covered with bark and placed on the side of an old oak tree from eight to ten feet from the ground are more likely to attract the nuthatch.

The nuthatch uses soft shreds of inner bark, rabbit fur, wool, cow hair, chicken feathers, pellets of dried earth, lumps of mud, small twigs, grasses, leaves, and rootlets for its nest materials.

One of its characteristics is to smear pitch just below the entrance hole or around it, even when building in a nesting box. Ornithologists are not certain of the true meaning of this. Perhaps it is related to keeping away other birds.

The incubation period of the nuthatch is approximately twelve days. Both parents incubate the eggs, five to ten in number, and the young remain in the nest for about two weeks after hatching. It raises one brood per year.

The nuthatch feeds on insects as well as vegetable matter, which includes nuts and acorns. It will devour hickory nuts, beechnuts, corn, and sunflower seeds. Its insect diet, mostly in spring and summer, includes beetles, spiders, caterpillars, tree bugs, ants, flies, grasshoppers, moths, millipedes, weevils, wood borers, treehoppers, plant lice, cankerworms, and many insect eggs.

The nuthatch is often called by such names as "upside-down bird", "devil down-head", "tree mouse", "topsy-turvy bird", and "black woodpecker".

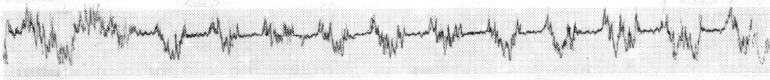

WHITE-BREASTED NUTHATCH

46

7.

HOUSE FINCH
(Carpódacus mexicánus)
length - 5½ to 6 inches

The word **finch** is from Middle English **finch, fynch,** Anglo-Saxon **finc,** Welch **pinc,** and Old English **chaffinc** (chaff plus finch: it eats chaff and grain). It was said to imitate its call-note (thought to sound like "fink" or "pink").

The house finch is an inhabitant of the west coast from British Columbia to southern Mexico as far east as western Nebraska. More commonly known as the linnet to many birders (Latin **linum,** feeding on flax seed from which linen was made), this little bird frequents streets of towns and cities across the west, along with the house sparrow, in search of food. It is said not to be popular with farmers and fruit growers because of its devastating tendencies and seems to be quite abundant throughout its range.

Beautifully plumaged, with bright red forehead, rump and breast, the male is easily detected among the flock. Its flanks are streaked with brown and its bright colors are more brilliant than its cousin, the purple finch. It breeds almost anywhere near water, constructing its nest in the eaves of buildings, forks of limbs, tin cans, pipes, old hats, or whatever else is available. Its habits are akin to those of the wren family. Attracted easily to man-made houses, most people consider it is a lovely bird to have around.

Ornithologists tell of the shipment east of these birds in 1940 under the labels of "Hollywood Finches". In violation of the International Migratory Bird Treaty Act, this traffic was swiftly brought to a close. To avoid prosecution, however, the dealers released their birds and the finches are now inhabitants along the eastern seaboard, particularly from New Jersey to Connecticut and are extending this range each year. It also has been introduced into Hawaii.

The female does not carry the red coloration of the male but does carry the brownish hue with vertically brown striped breast on grayish background. The wing marks of both are quite similar to other finches. The female, too, has a plain head without the eye stripe or dark mustache of the male.

Its song is a clear rolling warble that varies in pitch, with notes running together often. Its call note is a dull "chip" but is of cheerful and musical resonance.

The house finch will build in a man-made home that has a two inch entrance hole and is approximately six-by-six-by-twelve inches and placed at a height of ten to twelve feet from the ground. The house can be placed under the house eaves, on tree limbs of lower branches, on fence posts, in barns and garden houses, and in many other sites.

The materials used by the house finch for its nesting purposes includes grass stems, plant fibers, leaves, rootlets, twigs, hair, string, wool, feathers, and other local materials. It may even build on another birds existing nest.

The nest is built by the female almost entirely with little or no assistance from the male. The nest is usually about five inches in diameter and two to two and one-half inches deep. Nest building takes approximately four days with a longer period used when an early season of nesting begins.

2-6, 4-5 common; pale blue, almost white, thinly speckled with black

The incubation period averages about fourteen days with the young remaining on the nest for another fourteen to sixteen days before flying. The female alone performs the incubation. The female broods the young during the first few days after which both parents provide the food.

The eggs usually are deposited daily until the full compliment is reached and incubation takes place soon thereafter.

Two broods are normal but a larger or smaller number is also found on occasion.

The house finch shows a marked tendency to return to the same nest in subsequent years.

The vegetable matter diet of the house finch is quite varied, depending upon availability. Said to prefer seeds, it also will eat almost any fruit found in its nesting area. Weed seeds have been found to comprise about 85% of its diet with animal matter accounting for the remaining 15%. City finch dwellers will eat a variety of table refuse, including various fats.

Some birders consider this house finch to be as objectionable as the house sparrow because of many similar habits. However, it is a more beautiful bird and much neater in its nesting characteristics.

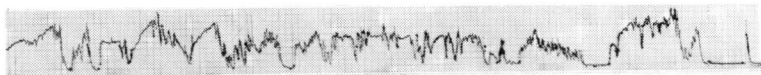

HOUSE FINCH

8.

HOUSE SPARROW (ENGLISH)
(Pásser doméesticus)
length - 5½ to 6½ inches

This is best known as a house sparrow to most of us. A rogue among birds, it is well described as abundant everywhere, building its nest of any available material and in any available place. Whether man wants this bird or not, he has it. Whether on the farm, in the city, in the town, or in the village, this little weaver finch will be around. Really not in the sparrow family but in the finch family, it is called by most people by many names — most of which are not tributes to the species. Old English for the word **sparrow** was **spearva**. Middle English was **sparive**, akin to Middle High German **sparwe** — all bird names for quiverer or flutterer, any of several old-world weaverbirds.

I have tried to reason with myself about accepting this bird and enjoying it. In fact, each year I reluctantly give up a couple of apartments in my purple martin house completely to it, hoping that one or two pairs of sparrows will keep the other sparrows from building. Sometimes this works, sometimes it doesn't. Not easily discouraged, it returns again and again. If it only would build a decent nest, but it doesn't! Never known to stop when the building

area is full, it persists in leaving something on the outside, usually an unsightly piece of scrap trailing downward, waving in the wind. You can always tell the bird lives there by the nesting materials that are left hanging outside.

Introduced into the United States from England in 1850, it became established, spread rapidly, and is now a serious pest. I recall reading that one ornithologist moved into a new neighborhood that seemingly was infested with house sparrows. He began a trapping campaign and after eliminating around two hundred of these birds, he noted little or no difference in the remaining population. Under such conditions what is man to do other than accept this bird as a resident?

However, there are some ways to discourage the sparrows. I have found that by eliminating as many nest building places as possible, the majority will be forced to go elsewhere to build. For example, a likely place is between the boards in the house louvers of your own house. By placing hardware cloth or screen wire across these, inside or outside, they will be eliminated as nesting sites. Greasing with clear lubricants other sloping areas, metal in particular, will assist in discouraging the house sparrow from lodging.

These little birds steal the food from the other species, oust our bluebirds, finches, martins, and other birds from their houses, and they seem to thrive on almost any kind of edible food.

Looking at the positive side, though, these birds add a lot of cheer with their series of musical chirps, "cheep, cheep, cheep...", and they, along with the other birds, do help to eradicate many harmful insects.

They have to be listed as house building birds and one need not try to describe the type of house they prefer - for they seem to have no preferences, just any house with large enough entrance hole. They will build in any type of house, wanted or unwanted. So, perhaps we need to try finding justification for accepting this "passer domesticus" - without, of course, encouraging its "increasing of the clan."

The nesting materials used by the sparrows include grass, hay, feathers, scraps from the trash can, paper, rags, twigs - almost anything. Both sexes participate in nest building.

These birds lay from four to seven eggs that are quite colorful. Incubation takes from eleven to thirteen days, and the young remain about fifteen days before flying. They raise five or six broods a year, accounting for their large population. If the nest is destroyed, the sparrow begins another immediately. I have watched one begin immediately after I had removed its nest and eggs from a purple martin apartment, even starting before I had put the ladder away.

They feed their young, even if they fall from the nest, following them wherever they go about on the ground.

The female is often confused with our other sparrows, especially during winter feeding at the feeders. The unstreaked, dingy breast, the bold eyeline, and the streaked back are markings to help us distinguish it from others. The male has a gray crown, chestnut colored nape, a black bib, and dull white cheeks.

This sparrow's food is principally seeds and grain but its insect diet consists of Japanese beetles, aphids, caterpillars, sow bugs, snails, and many other insects of its locality. In early spring, these birds spend long hours going along tree branches eating insects.

Some believe that its population is declining because of the decline of available food in the cities, as well as on the farm. Horse manure of city and town used to be a favorite of the sparrow for the seed content and the replacement of the horse by the automobile was thought to have had an effect upon the population. Those people that have house sparrows, though, are likely to take a different viewpoint from this.

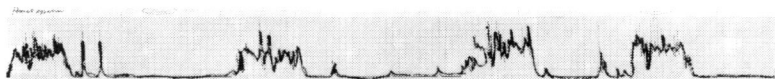

PHOTO BY DAVID G. ALLEN

HOUSE SPARROW

9.

SONG SPARROW
(Melospíza melódia)
length - 6 to 6¾ inches

The song sparrow is among our best known birds, summering across the northern half of the United States and southern Canada, it seldom builds its nest in the southern states, though a welcomed winter resident there.

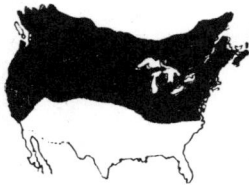

Its melodious song, often heard at night as well as during the daylight hours, is repeated as many as 300 times an hour. Because of its easily detected song notes, its melodious sound and its frequency, it has earned a place in much of literature.

Although relatively small in size and quite well marked in plumage, this heavily streaked bird with dark breast spots can be found in gardens, bushy fields, borders of creeks, lakes, and rivers across the northern states, both during winter and summer. It is often mistaken for the Savannah sparrow of similar markings. The fine streaks on the side of the crown and face, the streaks and stripes on its back, and profuse streaks on the breast assist in its identity. The sides of the throat and flank are dusky or somber in hue. There are many varieties or subspecies, depending upon the geographical area. For example, in the arid southwest it carries a much paler colored plumage, with minor size differences.

It is said that Thoreau rendered its long bright notes followed by short, trill ones in this lyric of merry music:

"Maids! maids! maids! hang up your teakettle-ettle-et-tle". At the close of summer its song becomes lower, slower and more warbled.

Its choosing bushes, hedgerows, and wood margins to nest in suggests that these are likely places to erect a manmade house. The house should be at least six inches in width, height, and depth and have all sides open. Locate it about two to three feet above ground, even within the hedge rows. Watch the chosen habitat of this bird and then be the judge of where to place the open shelf or "house".

This little sparrow builds its nest of grasses and rootlets and lines it with hair or other fine grasses. Its habit of building its nest on or near the ground, low in bushes or saplings, makes it an easy prey of roaming cats, snakes, and other predators.

The female alone incubates the eggs and the incubation period lasts for about twelve to fifteen days with the young ready to fly in another ten days. Should the young or the eggs fall victim to some cat, rat, snake or otherwise, the female builds another nest, often as many as four times, to rear one or two broods a season. It has been known to raise as many as four broods.

The cowbird, which does not build a nest of its own but simply lays its egg in among other laid bird eggs when the parent bird is away, often deposits its egg among those of the song sparrow. The sparrow then acts as foster parent and has been cited as raising as many as five of these cowbirds in one nest, to the detriment if not starvation of its own offspring.

The diet of the song sparrow includes weed seeds,

beetles, caterpillars, grasshoppers, and other insects.

This song sparrow is sometimes referred to as "ground bird", or "ground sparrow".

3-7, 4-6 common; varies from white to greenish blue spotted and speckled with brown .8 in. x .6 in.

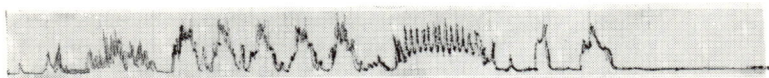

PHOTO BY DAVID G. ALLEN

SONG SPARROW

10.

PROTHONOTARY WARBLER
(Protonotária cítrea)
length - 5½ inches

The word warbler is from Middle English **werblen,** Old French **werbler** (meaning quaver with voice, to sing with trills and quavering, or to sing sweetly, trilly notes).

This colorful little beauty gets its name from the prothonotary who was the chief notary clerk or secretary in the College of Pro- thonotaries Apostolic in the early Anglican church who always wore a beautifully golden colored robe or vestment and it was given the name by the Creoles of Louisiana upon first find- ing them in the swampland.

The prothonotary is easily distinguished from all other warblers by his rich, brilliant yellow of the head and breast, sometimes almost orange or gold with only slightly paler color in the face, with no wing bars but a large amount of white in the tail area. Since this is perhaps the only warbler that seems to nest in man-made houses you are saved from trying to distinguish it from the forty species that occur in eastern United States. Identification of the various warblers poses a great problem for the beginning birder as well as the experienced one.

The habits in housing of this warbler resemble those of

the wrens, for they build in a variety of ways. It has been cited as building in many types of tree cavities of various sizes, in rotten stumps, under railroad bridges, in cigar boxes nailed on the wall, on pier tops, trestle-support beams, in bluebird houses, on railroad platforms, in tin cups in barns, in pasteboard boxes, fruit jars, paper sacks, pails hung on the wall, mail boxes, and many other types of structures. It fights with the wren for nesting places, which is quite understandable.

It prefers to be near water, being essentially a bird of the damp and swampy river bottoms and low-lying woods. Oaks, ashes, maples, elms, and other hardwoods seem to the liking of the prothonotary. The male selects the territory and at once attempts to drive off all opponents, if he is able to do so. He is a persistent singer, warbling from the time he arrives until he is successful in attracting his mate.

The call is a strong "tweet, tweet, tweet...", of about the same pitch.

In searching for a likely nesting site, the size and condition of the tree cavity seems to make little difference to this warbler. It matters not how large or how small the cavity is, he fills it regardless of the size and right up to the entrance hole. The old deserted woodpecker holes are favorite sites, particularly if near a stream or out in a lake or pond.

The nest is built almost entirely by the female, though the male uses the nest building technique to encourage her in mating.

The nest is made of soft green moss and a few fine roots, some dry leaves and cypress twigs. Sometimes feathers are found in the nest lining. The nest is about two inches in diameter and one and one half inches deep.

3-8, 4-6 common; creamy white heavily marked with brown or purple .75 in. x .5 in.

About ten days are required for nest construction.

Incubation takes from twelve to fourteen days and is done by the female, being fed by the male while she is on the nest. The young remain on the nest for another period of almost eleven days before being able to fly. Often two broods a year are raised.

The prothonotary warbler is a highly insectivorous bird, obtaining most of its food from the trunks of trees and branches of limbs as well as from fallen brush and old logs. Ants and other insect larvae are among its diet.

Its summer range is across the eastern half of the United States.

The nest is built at heights ranging from three feet to thirty-five or forty feet, but this warbler seems to prefer lower heights when they are available. The wren houses and bluebird houses are likely places for this warbler to build, also.

It is sometimes referred to as the "golden swamp warbler" and one can readily see why such a name could be used.

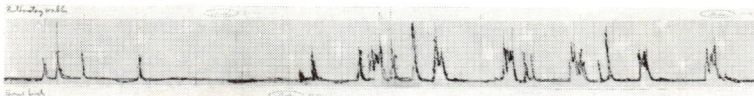

PROTHONOTARY WARBLER

11.

EASTERN BLUEBIRD
(Siália sialis)
length - 6¼ to 7 ¾ inches

This is one of our most beautiful birds, marked somewhat like the robin though much more colorful and much smaller. New Englanders, among our earlier settlers, referred to the bluebird as the "robin bird", for it reminded them of their robin redbreast in the mother country of England, although smaller.

The bluebird is making a comeback after almost disappearing, thanks to our well known bluebird devotees, especially Dr. Laurence Zeleny. Formerly plentiful across the eastern half of the United States, because of its nesting habits of using fence posts and easily accessible holes in the lower parts of dead trees, it has become less populous from year to year because of predators. Man, too, has depleted the forests that were used by this species, while cats and other stray animals sought out its nest for destruction of the young birds.

The adult bluebird has a solid blue back rusty reddish cinnamon throat and a dull white abdomen area. The wings are almost black at the tips.

It shuns the deep forests, preferring to build in open country, fence posts, backyard gardens, and the like. My first experience with a nesting pair was in my early youth

when I erected an apple box for a purple martin house. That year I had martins, bluebirds and house sparrows in the same birdbox. I well remember the melodious notes of the bluebird's sweet warbled "cherwee" song and its smooth velvety flight.

The winter season is its greatest enemy as it often perishes for lack of food. Frequently it does not go as far south as it should from northern climates and severe icy, wintry spells kill it off in larger numbers. Then, its migration pattern northward in spring when begun too early, at times causes a similar devastation.

The house sparrow (weaver finch) also has taken a toll of bluebirds as it crowded out the bluebird from its nesting box or other site.

For the bluebird fancier, there is no more beautiful sight than a pair of bluebirds at mating time. The male, as is usual with most species, begins to arrive a bit early, selects the nesting site, locates his mate, and then begins to convince his mate to take up abode in the site that he has found. He carols his sweetest, most seductive notes day after day in his attempted attraction. When finally successful, he displays his charms further by spreading his tail feathers, lowering his halfopened wings and warbling soft undertones to secure her favor. Finally, when successful with his wooing techniques, he leads her to the selected nesting site, looks in and tries to entice her to venture inside. Sometimes, this nuptial affair is joined by another female or another male. Such trespassing means a conflict is on, soon settled, though, as only a single pair will remain.

3-8, 5 common; pale blue, sometimes white, unmarked .9 in. x .7 in.

Widespread use of insecticides by man has also taken its toll of bluebirds, as has the encroachment of the starling.

The bluebird house should be placed from six to twelve feet high. It is important to make the house deep enough to prevent the raccoon, owl, cat or other predator from reaching inside to disturb the nest, eggs, adults or the young birds. An opening of one and one half inches will be satisfactory. The boxes should not be placed too close together; two hundred feet or more apart is suggested. On occasions bluebirds will build in houses that are closer together, however. One birder spoke of having a wren box hanging from a tree limb about fifty feet from where there was a bluebird box on a pole, and in between was a feeder. The bluebirds built in all three. Another bluebird fancier has told me of having several pairs of bluebirds nesting in her martin house. These are notable exceptions, however.

Still another birder has cited using a milk carton covered with contact paper that had a wooded pattern on it and nailed to a fence post. A brood was raised in one of these. Hanging houses from limbs of trees will be accepted by bluebirds sometimes.

Bluebird houses should be monitored frequently during nesting season. The flying squirrel, a nocturnal animal seldom seen during the day, often goes into bluebird houses during the nesting season to raise a family of squirrels. If such occurs, then you must decide whether to let the squirrel raise its family and erect another bluebird box nearby or remove the squirrel before he raises his family. Perhaps erecting another bluebird house would be the best decision.

The bluebird forms its nest of dried grasses and weed stems, carelessly arranged. The nest is poorly and loosely structured with occasional use of fine twigs and still finer grass for the lining of the nest. Sometimes a little hair and small amount of feathers are found inside the nest.

Both sexes help in building the nest which usually takes between four and twelve days. The materials used are those found within close proximity with the female performing almost all of the work of collecting nesting materials.

Incubation takes about twelve days and the young remain in the nest for fifteen to eighteen days. Incubation is performed mainly by the female with occasional assistance from the male. Both parents feed the young. Two and sometimes three broods a season are found.

The bluebirds are among our most useful birds, destroying large quantities of insects. Stomach examinations by ornithologists show that about 68% of their food is animal and 32% vegetable. Grasshoppers, crickets, katydids, beetles, ants, stink bugs, chinch bugs, drone bees, caterpillars, moths, spiders, sowbugs, snails, and angel wings were found in varying degrees, with the grasshoppers, crickets, and katydids making up the preponderous part of the diet.

Vegetation included wild fruits, seeds from sumacs, poison ivy seeds and bayberries.

The bluebird is often referred to as "little robin", "blue robbie", and "little mister blue".

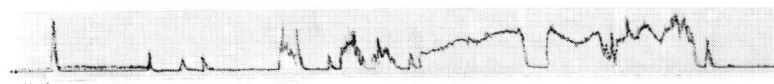

WESTERN BLUEBIRD
(Siália mexicána)
about the same size

The western cousin is very much like the eastern bluebird. The same in size and general colorations, this western one has a rusty red upper back color not found on the eastern one. In other words, the top and bottom colors are reversed. Otherwise, they are alike and not easily told apart.

Its habits are very similar to the eastern bluebird and it, too, is easily attracted to man-made houses but must defend its territory from the violet green swallow and the wrens.

PHOTO BY DAVID G. ALLEN

EASTERN BLUEBIRD

12.

BARN SWALLOW
(Hirúndo rústica)
length - 5¾ to 7¾ inches

The word **swallow** is from Middle English **swalwen,** Old English **swealwe** or **swelgan,** Icelandic **svala** and German **schwalbe** — referring to small, swift-flying insect eating birds.

The barn swallow is one of the birds that prefers a shelf upon which to build. It is the only swallow with a deeply forked tail, an excellent identification feature to distinguish it from other swallows during the migration period.

It breeds across most of North America, only the extreme southeastern part having few or no summer residents.

Its graceful flight is admired by all, along with its plumage and forked tail. The farmer knows this bird well, since it flies in and out of his sheds and barns, building its nest on ledges, rafters, and similar places. The modern farmer, though, with less open buildings is not likely to see these pleasant summer dwellers unless he supplies them with supports for their nests as well as an entrance to his barns and houses.

The dull dark back adds to this swallow's beauty as its spring arrival occurs, in transit gracefully skimming low over fields and ponds seeking insects or nesting sites.

As is typical of the swallow family, this species often arrives too early and an unexpected cold spell prevents it from getting enough insects to sustain it until the inclement weather is over, often killing many. Two or three such freezing days can cause this to happen. It is then that man can assist by opening his garage and barn doors and windows to permit these birds to have a safe place in order to survive.

The soft, twittering song of "kvik, kvik, wit, wit" is a commonly heard summer call of this species.

Since the barn swallow prefers a shelf, man can assist by providing a two by four joist, unplaned and unpainted, nailed to the wall of the outside of the house or building, placed up under the eaves with five or six inches of clearance above. From eight to twelve feet above the ground is recommended, though greater heights will also be accepted.

This graceful bird builds its nest of mud mixed with pieces of grass. An excellent mason, using his bill for a trowel, he begins with a mud base for attaching to the wall board or shelf, then weaves grasses into the mud as the nest grows higher and higher. At it takes shape, larger and longer pieces of grass and straw are used until the final cup is made and the nest is often lined with feathers. If near the coast, seaweed is often used; if near available feathers, more of these will be found in the lining of the nest. White poultry feathers are a preferred item.

The nest of the barn swallow has been found on the outside of wharf buildings, boats, boat houses, in vacant houses, under the eaves of dwellings, the iron rail of a hay rack, a loop of rope, an iron hoop, an open joist or beam. One observer noted as many as twenty-seven nests in a single barn; however, four or five are more typical.

3-6
white, spotted
with brown
.8 in. x .5 in.

Both sexes work together to build the nest, taking approximately eight days to complete it.

The swallow returns to the same nesting site from year to year.

While considered a gentle, harmless creature, tending to its own business and seldom, if ever, bothering its neighbor, the barn swallow will defend its nesting territory against intrusion from other swallows and the eastern phoebe, a great competitor.

The period of incubation is from fifteen to seventeen days. Both sexes share the responsibility. Two broods are raised in the temperate range.

The young remain in the nest another eighteen to twenty-three days, being fed constantly by both male and female. As the period ends, the young are enticed from the nest by the parents discontinuing their feeding. As they do, both parents fly back and forth near the nest to further encourage the young to fly.

After the young make their first flight, they remain in the vicinity for a few days, returning to the nest each night.

Some observers have reported that the parents feed the young after they are able to fly. This takes place on the wing, while the young sit on a tree limb, or on wires.

The juvenile plumage is very much like the adult but duller and paler. Both sexes look alike and the richer, brighter colors of adulthood are observed only when they arrive the next year from their sojourn to the south for the winter months.

The adult has a blue-black hue above, cinnamon-buff

below, a darker throat area and white tail spots.

The barn swallow's food is practically 100% animal matter. Stomach examinations revealed about 99% animal matter and 1% vegetable matter. Flies of various kinds seemed to be a preference, with beetles, weevils, ants, bees and wasps eaten to a lesser degree. Grasshoppers, stink bugs, leaf bugs, plant lice, chinch bugs, crickets, dragon flies, May flies, spiders, and snails have been found in a limited number. The very small vegetable diet was accounted for in elderberries and some wheat kernels.

The barn swallow can be seen following the farmers plow, skimming across the ground devouring such insects as are stirred up.

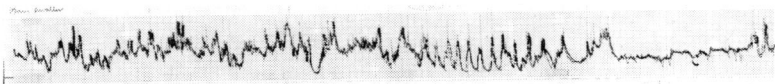

BARN SWALLOW

13.

TREE SWALLOW
(Iridoprócne bícolor)
length - 5 to 6¼ inches

The only green-backed swallow nesting in the eastern part of the United States, it prefers to frequent the New England area, although it is a winter visitor in southern United States. It may be confused in winter time with the rough-winged swallow but its white feathers extend above the tail, giving it a mark of distinction. Traveling in huge flocks, it leaves its southern winter habitat for a trip to the north, finally nesting as far north as Alaska.

A seed eater as well as an insect eater, its favorite seed is the bayberry. Often it maneuvers close to the winter ice or snow for food. It also gathers seeds on the wing as it wends its way northward, following the course of a river, flying low as it gathers food.

The tree swallow has a blue-black or green-black plumage above and a clear white hue below. The immature is a dusky brown above.

I have seen as many as thirty of these birds flying about two or three feet above the ground in a grassy cloverleaf highway exchange, catching insects during a spring migration northward. Their green backs attested to their identity, since the similarly colored violet-green swallow does not migrate across eastern United States.

Known to eat more vegetable matter than any other swallow, it has a built-in advantage for cold weather that other swallows do not have, thus enabling it to stay north if it prefers, or at least longer than other swallows.

It is an early morning singer with a sweet, rapid variation of "weet, trit, weet".

The tree swallow has been found to quickly appropriate purple martin sites and bluebird sites but still builds in old apple orchards and holes in trees, especially when they are near meadows or bodies of water. The tree swallows commonly nest in isolated pairs and show little of the communal habits of the purple martin and cliff swallow. They do nest in single boxes or boxes placed not far apart, thus showing some of the communal instincts. Perhaps this is due to a common feeding area more than a desire to be together at nesting time.

The house should have a one and one-half inch diameter entrance and should be placed from ten to fifteen feet above the ground, near water if possible, and in an open area. These birds have been known to select unusual nesting sites, such as a woodpecker den, a hole in piling of an old wharf, cavities in eaves of houses, cornices of barns, and in fence posts beside the road.

The nest is made of an accumulation of dry grass and straw, hollowed out and lined with feathers, often white ones, and placed so that the nest extends upward over the eggs during incubation. The female builds the nest, aided little or not at all by the male.

Incubation takes from twelve to sixteen days and the young remain on the nest for another sixteen to twenty-four days. The male seldom performs any incubation duties but will take insects to the female while she is on the nest. The male does not share the house at night, although he does stay on top the dwelling until after darkness, seemingly as a protector or just nearby partner.

The young are strong of wing when they leave the nest, "taking to the air like veterans", accompanied by both parents. Only one brood is raised each year.

4-6
white, unmarked
.7 in. x .6 in.

The sexes are much alike in appearance and the young take on their adult plumage by winter season, thus making it quite difficult to distinguish the young from mature birds.

The tree swallow, as has been noted, differs from the other American swallows in that it eats more vegetable matter. Examination of stomachs have shown their contents to include about 80 percent animal matter and 20 percent vegetable matter. The vegetable matter was made up of various seeds and fruits but the bayberry or waxberry seemed to be its choice. The animal matter consisted mainly of beetles, mosquitos, flies, ants and gnats. Minor items included grasshoppers, dragon flies, and spiders. Others have found the diet to also include crustacean forms and water spiders. Bulrush, sedge, smartweed, and fragments of rose thorns were among the vegetable matter eaten.

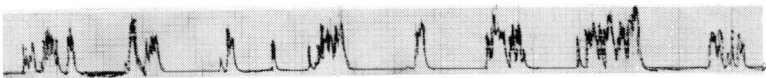

TREE SWALLOW

14.
VIOLET-GREEN SWALLOW
(Tachycinéta thalassina)
length - 5½ inches

The violet-green swallow is one of our most beautiful birds of the swallow family. Clearly distinguishable by its velvety hues of violet and green on its upper surface and its white flank patches below that almost meet over the tail, it can only be confused with the tree swallow which has the same green back. When seen in flight, both have white underpinnings but a view from above would clearly show the difference as one views the white areas. Identification poses a great problem for those persons living west of the Rockies where both species are found but is no problem for those living east of the Rockies because the violet-green swallow does not frequent that area.

My attention was once drawn to these beautiful birds when on a summer vacation trip to a mountain resort area just west of Boulder, Colorado, where almost every summer cabin had swallow occupants in its bird house. This was a beautiful sight to observe.

The flight pattern of the violet-green is somewhat different from the tree swallow. The violet-green swallow seems to flap its wings more rapidly and to glide less than the tree swallow. Both have similar habits in general, however.

The violet-green swallow frequents mountain heights

and it is easily attracted to single room houses which should have a one and one-half inch diameter entrance hole. These birds are often more populous than available housing. This almost assures a landlord of attracting these swallows if he provides a house.

Weather is its greatest enemy, with the population being decimated in large numbers in spring and fall during unusual weather conditions. This is commonly found among all swallows that are dependent almost entirely upon insect life for sustenance. At such times, when insects cannot be found, it becomes impossible for the swallows to obtain sufficient nourishment and many perish.

Seemingly unafraid of man, it takes up with almost any type of house, even known to build its nest under house eaves. It also builds in deserted woodpecker holes, natural cavities of trees, cracks, crevices, or holes in various kinds of mountainous cliffs. A box placed under the eaves of the house will be likely to attract the violet-green swallow as will houses erected on poles. One violet-green swallow landlord mentioned tossing out feathers into the air at nesting time to see these birds swoop down and snatch the feathers before they had wafted to the ground.

During nest building time these swallows have been observed to work at a leisurely pace, often taking as much as three weeks to complete their nests, with a waiting period of an additional few days.

Its nest is made of straw and dry grass, bits of string, and lined with feathers and horsehair, if available.

The call is a soft "chip" or "chit, chit", becoming shriller and faster at mating season and usually heard in early morning hours.

4-7, 4-5 common;
white, unmarked
.72 in. x .5 in.

The incubation period is thirteen to fourteen days with another ten day period before the young can fly. Upon flying they remain near the nest for a few more days and then disappear from the locality, only infrequently seen thereafter for the remainder of the season.

The young will often occupy a nearby telephone or electric light line while learning to fly. Frequently the adults will feed the young while they sit on the wires. This offers an interesting view to observe.

The female has been observed to do most of the feeding of the young with the male only occasionally bringing in something to eat.

Apparently only one brood is raised during a season, but a second attempt has been noticed when the first one failed for some reason.

Like swallows in general, the violet-green one catches insects on the wing, making these its principal diet, if not its entire diet. Stomach examinations have revealed the contents to include leafhoppers and leafbugs principally with flies, ants, wasps, and wild bees found in small quantities. Other insects common to the particular area will also be a part of the diet.

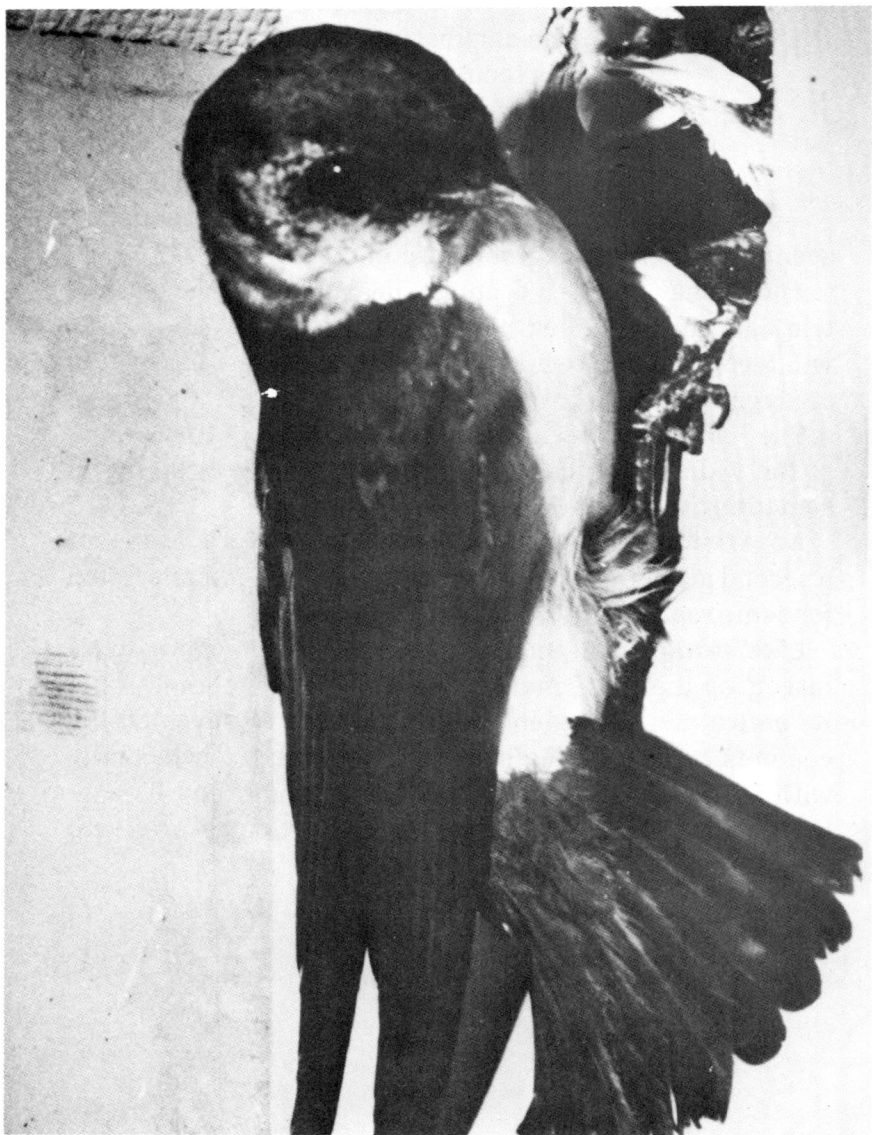

VIOLET GREEN SWALLOW

15.

PURPLE MARTIN
(Prógne súbis)
length - 7¼ to 8½ inches

The word **martin** is a male Christian name common in western Europe, after St. Martin, bishop of Tours. The name is applied in French to a number of various birds. The application of the Christian name to the bird has no obvious reason and may have been purely arbitrary. Many writers of the 17th century say that the martin is so called because it comes in March and departs about Martinmas (festival of St. Martin, November 11).

The purple martin is the largest of the swallow family and is indeed a friend of man. Perhaps this all-American bird is the one attracted more than any other to man-made bird houses. A colony bird, never liking to live alone, it can be attracted to many varieties of houses.

In historic times this bird built its nest in cavities of trees, in cliffs, caves, and later in gourds put up by the Indians and continued to this day by some martin lovers. Farmers have had purple martins for years as protectors of their young chickens, for the purple martin attacks birds of prey whenever they come near the nesting area. This writer has witnessed this on many occasions.

The martin wends its way in spring to every state in the

United States and across all of the provinces of Canada — even into Alaska, where it has been cited as nesting not too far from the latitude of the Arctic Circle.

There is nothing that will make a martin birder leap from his bed faster than the first twitter of the male scout in spring, for he knows then that his birds are back for another year after a winter sojourn in South America where they bask in the sunny skies of South American countries and islands along the northern coast of South America and as far south as São Paulo, Brazil.

Arrival in spring is usually first by the male scout who soon leaves abruptly to search out his mate elsewhere. Some say that the male flies back to South America to get his mate. This is very doubtful. More likely she is among those at a communal roosting area somewhere in the not too far distant environs further south.

The song of the purple martin is a series of rich gurgling notes of varying pitch, often ending with a rattling gurgle. It is distinctive and easily discerned from other birds.

When the female(s) arrives, a bit of courting takes place as the male seeks to attract as many to the house as he can and to fend off other males if possible, though he soon tires and permits other males and females aboard also.

The purple martin is an insect eater almost entirely. Seldom has the diet been found to contain vegetable matter. A favorite insect of the martin is the mosquito and the martin eradicates more than his share of this pest.

3-7, 5 common;
white, unmarked
1 in. x .7 in.

Because of this bird's fondness for mosquitos man has been encouraged to erect martin houses. Commercial ventures for martin house sales have promoted "2000 mosquitos a day" and this could be a possibility. Regardless of the exact number, however, some martin lovers will swear that they have not had a mosquito on their premises since they got purple martins. To say the least, the purple martin does eradicate many harmful insects. For this reason alone it is a desirable bird. More so, though, for its beautiful purplish-black color, its acrobatics in entertainment, and its beautiful song, it has become an accepted yard bird everywhere.

This is one bird that requires little or no attention from man after the house is erected. The apartment house or the gourd-cluster should be cleaned out annually, however, sprayed or dusted for mites, repaired, repainted and erected again at arrival time the following spring.

Scented cedar chips and cedar boughs dusted with sulphur dust and placed in each apartment or each gourd may control the mite problem and help to discourage the sparrow and starling. Cut the cedar foliage into small pieces about one half inch long or smaller and place about half a cupful in each apartment. If the house is erected too early in the spring, the sparrows or starlings are likely to take over. Many landlords wait until the male scouts have been sighted in the area before erecting the martin house. This keeps the sparrow, a persistent, perpetual builder, from claiming the house before the martins arrive. Some martin fanciers recommend lowering the house again, or plugging the holes, after the scout leaves and not erecting it or not opening the holes again until the arrival of male and female later. If this procedure is followed, one should be alert to the second arrival time so that the house can be erected or opened immediately; otherwise, he stands the chance of the birds going on to another complex of apartments.

The same birds often come back to the same house and apartment from year to year, proven by bird banding.

The greatest enemies of the purple martin are cold weather, tornadoes, hurricanes, snakes, and squirrels. To protect the house from predator enemies the house should be erected at least thirty feet from trees and at a height of fourteen to twenty feet above the ground. An open front free of buildings, trees, poles, or wires is preferred so the birds can swoop in without interference. Some people make the mistake of erecting their houses sufficiently far from trees but then plant bushes and shrubs underneath the house and around the pole. This will offend the martins, for they are leery of a snake abiding there.

Care should be taken to place a barrier or guard on the pole to prevent snakes and squirrels from climbing the pole and it is well to remember that both can climb metal poles as well as wooden ones. A greased section of pole will discourage the snake but not the squirrel. Whether you use metal, plastic, or wooden houses or use plastic or natural gourds, these should be provided in a colony type. Do not begin with less than four apartments and do not try to continue adding apartments after you have a house full of birds. Leave some for others to attract.

Longevity of the purple martin is at least thirteen years and nine months, shown by a banded dead purple martin found by researchers.

The martin nest is made of dead twigs from nearby trees, pine straw, hay, grasses, and other nearby objects. The nest may be lined with leaves and rootlets, no structure of beauty, but functional. A bit of mud is often placed at the entrance hole, perhaps a carry-over from the early days of cave or cliff nest-site building, to keep the eggs from rolling out of the nest, or just because it is a swallow and this is a common trait among swallows.

Incubation is from twelve to twenty days, the average being thirteen or fourteen days. The female performs the incubation but both sexes feed the young. During the early or middle summer when the eggs are incubating, one of the adult birds will often go and procure a green leaf from a tree and place it over the eggs, perhaps to cool them somewhat during the extreme heat period. After hatching, the young remain on the nest for three to four weeks. After flying, the young return to the house for a few days and then all depart. Only one brood is raised each year.

One of the most entertaining observations is to watch the feeding of the young, especially during dragon fly season, when the young attempt to swallow the large flies. A young martin may appear to be a bird from another world or as if a miniature airplane is about to take off.

The insect diet of the purple martin includes mosquitos, flies, treehoppers, black bugs, beetles, moths, butterflies, dragon flies, and other local insects.

The young male and female look alike with a dull light gray color below and light gray forehead, and appear so until their first post-nuptial molt, about the 18th month. This means that the young may reappear as adults all looking like females for the next season, raise a brood without the human landlord thinking he is observing a single male available. In this case, he is not aware of this late post nuptial molt time. It is only after this time that the male adult takes on the full dark purplish-black plumage all over. Therefore the typical martin lover will never be able to look at his birds and say for sure that he has a certain number of males and females for there will always be some young adult birds amid the group among which he cannot distinguish male from female.

Perhaps the weather is the greatest enemy of the purple martin and it is something that man can do nothing about.

Sometimes an early arrival of these birds followed by an extremely cold spell that lasts for about a week can be devastating to the purple martin, killing off many because of the lack of insects for sustenance. Some martin landlords have found that placing a piece of suet into which crickets can be placed will be accepted by this bird during these extreme weather conditions. This suet combination can be elevated to the house porch by using a long cane pole and raking the mixture from the end of the pole. It would certainly be worth trying, should your birds arrive and a severe cold snap follow.

Another weather pattern that decimates the purple martins by the thousands is the fall hurricanes. The hurricanes are coming up from the south across the Gulf of Mexico as the martins are leaving toward the south across the same area. When the two occur simultaneously, the hurricane usually wins and devastation of bird life follows. Of course there is nothing that one can do about this. It should be noted, though, that this may explain to landlords why their birds do not return one year. Hurricane Camille is a good example of fall weather devastation of bird life among the migratory species. When this devastation of bird life occurs, it usually takes several years for them to build back again to their former population.

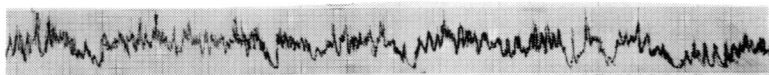

PURPLE MARTIN

16.

DOWNY WOODPECKER
(Dendrócopos pubéscens)
length - 6¼ to 7¼ inches

The downy woodpecker gets its name of **downy** because of its soft, fine feathers. The downy, smallest of the family of woodpeckers, is frequently seen in almost every state as well as southern Canada. This is not a shy bird in the least and will readily come to the backyard feeders to eat suet and varied bird seeds.

The downy is often confused with the hairy woodpecker, since their markings are quite similar. Both range across the same territory except for the lower southwest where the downy is less often seen. The downy is somewhat smaller than the hairy in size and when the two are seen separately it is not always easy to distinguish them one from the other. The short, stubby bill of the downy is a good way to distinguish it from the hairy and perhaps will give the best clue to look for. I had difficulty remembering which one is the smaller of the two but found that by using this neumonic device I could always recall. By associating downy (down) with small it becomes easy to remember. The downy is the smaller of the two.

The downy is most likely to be the one that you see at the feeder, since the hairy keeps more to the forest than the downy. However, I have had both feeding at my feeders during the winter months, on the suet cakes especially.

The tail, wings, and back of both downy and hairy woodpeckers have a black hue, intermingled with white spots. A black cap adorns each, below which there is a white stripe. A small scarlet patch appears at the nape of the neck. A black stripe runs through the eye and another white stripe is below this. The female does not have the scarlet patch. The downies have barred outer tail feathers not found on the hairies.

The downy likes the open woodlands and not the densely forested regions — thus making it more readily attracted to human dwelling sites. It is often a nester in city parks.

The courtship of the downy is much akin to the flicker, the courting pair chasing each other from tree to tree, almost constantly on the move. An interesting sight is to watch the male drumming on a tree, then looking around for his attracted mate-to-be. It is thought that he alone is the drummer of the species and what one might interpret to be the female responding is, instead, another male attempting to enter the scene.

The male and female in courting season will weave head and body from side to side both while perching on horizontal limbs or on the trunks of trees. Their heads are held with bills in line with the body as they brace with their tails and perform for one another. They may sail from tree to tree during mating, uttering their low, harsh, chattering cry of "peek, peek".

The downy woodpecker house should be about five inches in interior diameter with a depth of six to ten inches. The entrance hole should be about one and one fourth inches in diameter and the house should be placed anywhere from eight to forty feet high. On the side of a dead tree is an excellent place to locate the house. This bird makes the entrance hole a geometrical circle when building his own house, not living in one made for him by man.

4-6
white, unmarked
.8 in. x .6 in.

When building its own tree-home and nest, the downy woodpecker uses a small portion of wood shavings that have fallen inside. Most of the chips are taken away by both male and female. Too, seldom do the downies, like other woodpeckers, use the same nesting hole and cavity year after year. Instead, the site is taken over the next year by chickadees, titmice, tree swallows, wrens, and sometimes by bluebirds. Both male and female tend to the nest making, such as it is.

The incubation period is about twelve days with the young remaining for about ten to twelve days more. Feeding the young is by both male and female with regurgitation of food for the first four or five days, followed by insect feeding. Only one brood is raised.

Animal matter makes up about three-fourths of the downy's diet, with vegetable matter the other fourth. Animal matter consists of ants, spiders, snails, beetles, weevils, and caterpillars, with other local insects included. Its vegetable diet is mostly of useless wild varieties.

It is commonly referred to as "little downy", or just "downy".

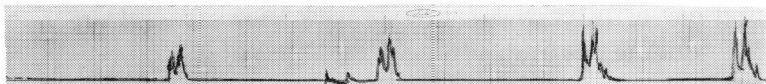

DOWNY WOODPECKER

17.

HAIRY WOODPECKER
(Dendrócopos villósus)
length - 8½ to 10½ inches

The hairy woodpecker, a more retiring forest lover, is not likely to be seen at your backyard feeder as much as its cousin downy. It will come, but not as readily.

Its summer area is largely in deciduous woods, old orchards, or borders of wooded areas. Those persons having a wooded area on their premises are more likely to attract the hairy woodpecker.

It can be distinguished from the like patterned downy woodpecker through its size, much larger, and mainly by its bill, which is longer, less stubby than the downy's and its bill is about as long as its head.

Both hairy and downy have similar markings (see downy), with a broad white patch extending down the back and stripes on the wings. The sexes are similar in coloration except for the absence of the red patch on the back of the head of the female. Since there are several geographic varieties of the hairy woodpecker, some variation in size and coloration may be found.

Its call is a loud "peek" or "pluk" and a rapid rattling sound, somewhat like the kingfisher. It, too, drums on a limb or the trunk of a tree during mating season. Also, its drumming can be heard in midwinter — perhaps to delineate its territory or just to see what response it can get.

Rarely is the hairy woodpecker seen in the highlands but is abundant in the swamplands, often nesting in a dead tree whose base is water covered.

The house of the hairy woodpecker should have a one and one-half inch entrance hole and should be placed on the side of a dead tree or one that is dying. Placement on an otherwise nearby tree may also attract this little woodpecker, especially if the tree is on the edge of a stream. An old decaying orchard tree, apple, pear, or peach, may be a likely spot. The house should be placed from five to thirty feet above the ground. The floor should be covered with wood shavings to a depth of one to two inches.

The hairy woodpecker, like others in the woodpecker family, uses a few shavings of its own making. It is not usually observed taking in any outside nesting materials.

Only one brood is raised in a season, but the hairy woodpecker will lay a second set of eggs if the first set is robbed or destroyed. It has been known to lay even a third set.

Both sexes incubate the eggs for about fourteen days. When the young are hatched they are fed by regurgitation of food by the parents until the young are able to reach their heads out of the hole. Feeding continues then with insects and vegetation for a total time of about twenty-one days.

Like its cousin downy, about seventy-five percent of the diet is insect life, particularly the injurious type of insects.

Insects eaten include spiders, ants, caterpillars, wood boring types, aphids, grasshoppers, crickets, cockroaches, and beetles. Its twenty-five percent vegetable diet consists of weed seeds, wild fruits, and nuts (acorns, hazlenuts, and beechnuts primarily). This bird is of inestimable value to both farmer and city dweller for the tremendous insect life that it devours.

3-6, 4 common;
white to orange pink
.85 in. x .65 in.

The hairy woodpecker is usually referred to as "hairy", "little hairy", "hairy woodpecker", "sapsucker", or "big sapsucker".

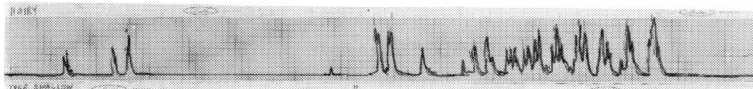

96

HAIRY WOODPECKER

18.

GOLDEN-FRONTED WOODPECKER
(Centúrus aúrifrons)
length - 8½ to 14½ inches

This woodpecker is found more in Mexico than in the United States. However, the golden fronted woodpecker does extend its summer range northward into south-central Texas, perhaps as far north as the southwestern boundary of Oklahoma. It is often found with the red-bellied woodpecker where the two territories overlap, but the red-bellied covers most of the eastern half of the United States. Both are similar in general appearance. The orange nape patch of the golden fronted species distinguishes it from the red nape of the red-bellied one. Also, there is a yellow spot just above the bill of the golden fronted woodpecker where the red-bellied has a red spot. Otherwise, the two are about the same size and with similar color characteristics, black and white barred back, red cap, brownish red to gray belly, and white rump patch.

This species was slaughtered in large numbers in lower Texas during the advent of the telephone and telegraph line construction because of their attacks upon the soft pine poles erected for the lines. This caused a radical decrease in the population of the species.

They are not shy birds but will readily visit yards and orchards. Open deciduous or mixed coniferous woodlands are choice areas, as well as oak and elm trees along river banks and around lakes and ponds. In town they take readily to shade trees and dead trees. They have been known to build in man-made bird houses of the flicker type, especially when the dead tree of a former nesting site has been removed or has been blown down.

Formerly nesting in Florida and other southern states, their habitat is now confined primarily to a part of Texas and farther south into Mexico.

The call of this woodpecker resembles that of other woodpeckers, especially the flicker and the red-bellied and is a series of scolding, harsh calls of "cher-r-r..." and "wicka-wicka-wicker" - often varied.

The house for the golden fronted woodpecker should resemble as much as possible a dead tree section. Perhaps the best structure is a cross-section of a dead tree about eight to ten inches in diameter with a two inch entrance hole, preferably a section of a fallen tree with an existing woodpecker hole of two inch size. It should be attached to the side of a dead tree if possible, or an oak, elm, hackberry, ash, hickory, or even a tall fence post properly located.

While a height of twelve to twenty feet above the ground level is suggested, a likely higher location will also serve, since the species sometimes builds as far up as seventy feet with about forty feet being its more expected height extreme.

Like other woodpeckers it uses inside chips cut while excavating its hole. A small amount of chips of the mentioned hardwoods may be placed in the bottom of the tree section of the house before you erect it.

3-8, 4-5 common;
white
1 in. x .8 in.

Incubation takes about fourteen days with both sexes assisting. Both sexes also tend to the feeding of the young birds.

As many as three broods have been known to be raised by the golden-fronted woodpecker in some instances, though this is deemed exceptional.

These birds are cited as persistent layers. If the first set of eggs is destroyed, a second set will be laid within a span of a week or two and at the same site.

The diet of this woodpecker consists of about 75% animal matter and 25% vegetable matter. Animal matter is composed of ants, beetles, caterpillars, crickets, spiders, different kinds of flies, and larvae of various insects. Small frogs have been found in various instances. Vegetable matter included acorns, beechnuts, pine seeds, juniper berries, wild grapes, blackberries, strawberries, pokeberries, palmetto berries, sour gum berries, cherries, apples, oranges, mulberries, elderberries, bayberries, Virginia creeper berries, cornel, holly, dogwood and poison ivy berries, ragweed seeds, wild sasparilla, hazelnuts and pecans. This woodpecker, too, stores food for future use.

PHOTO BY F. G. IRWIN, CORNELL UNIV.

GOLDEN-FRONTED WOODPECKER

19.

RED-HEADED WOODPECKER
(Melanérpes erythrocéphalus)
length - 8¼ to 9¾ inches

I have often thought how nice it would be if this bird had been our national bird, except for the fact that it seldom is seen in the western states. The red, white, and blue colors of the red-headed woodpecker make it easy to identify.

Formerly seen on top of almost every telephone pole and light pole with its nesting entrance hole easily in view, it later became necessary for the redhead to move to the woodlands as man replaced these untreated poles with creosote, chemically treated ones, or with metal poles. As a boy I counted thirty-six nesting holes in poles along streets within two miles of our home. This same area now has none.

The red-headed is one of our most beautiful birds, both in flight and at rest on a tree trunk or limb. A pair nest each year across the lake behind the house, high up in a dying sycamore on the edge of the lake and during the nesting season this pair command the tree, only giving way to others during other seasons. It is quite interesting to watch the change of command of this treetop from season to season throughout the year.

The red-headed woodpecker dwells in open woodlands, not frequenting dense forest growth. It likes a dead or dying tree that is on or near a lakeside, creek, or river bank. Burned over areas are a particular delight to him.

Its markings are distinct and easily recognizable, a brilliant red head and neck, with white rump, breast and lower wing tips outlined in a beautiful blue which covers the top two-thirds of the wing area.

Perhaps our most domesticated woodpecker, this friendly bird is easily attracted to your feeders, especially in very cold weather. Corn bread is one of its delights as well as ears of corn nailed to the side of a tree in the yard along with suet, the favorite of almost every species of bird. A corn tree made of ears of corn thrust upon spikes sticking out from a post will be a delight to this bird. After he has disposed of all the grains, the cob can then be removed and another one thrust in its place. These corn trees can be placed in various locations about the yard and in different patterns, designs and quantities. If not a cob spike tree, then a single spike will do.

City parks are a likely dwelling place for the red-headed woodpecker, especially parks of open, deciduous woods. These park areas provide a place to visit and observe this beautiful species.

Its song is sometimes referred to as a scolding series of syllables, "chur, chur" or "char, char".

This woodpecker's house with a two inch diameter entrance hole should be placed at heights of five to eighty feet above the ground. This wide range permits you to seek out a dead tree or dying tree in a somewhat open area, or one with bark off, and attach the house to the tree trunk. If possible, observe the location of the bird hole in a tree or pole elsewhere, perhaps at the city park, and try to duplicate this situation on your own premises. If the entrance hole was above a limb, then locate your house in a similar position.

4-7, common; white, unmarked 1.0 in. x .8 in.

The red-headed woodpecker usually nests in the dead tops of deciduous trees, in old oak limb stubs or tree stumps of ash, elm, sycamore, cottonwood, willow, as well as other hardwood trees. It has also been known to build in odd sites such as the hub of a farm wheel discarded from a wagon, a hole in an old pump on the farm, common fence posts, and idle farm instruments. Because of these offerings, the farmer may have greater potential in attracting these birds than the city family, but this species is just as prevalent in village, town and city.

The chiseled chips from the inner walls of the cavity are the nesting materials of the redhead. So, if you provide some shavings in the bottom of your bird house, about two inches deep will do, it may provide an added incentive for attracting this beautiful woodpecker. Sawdust is not as preferred as shavings that are a bit larger which often can be procured from the sawmill or the neighborhood high school industrial arts shop which nearly always daily discards such shavings from the planer. Or, you may make your own with a knife or chisel. These can be made from any of the hardwoods mentioned previously.

Incubation lasts for about two weeks. Both sexes assist in the incubation and also in feeding the young. Some birders have observed that an egg a day is layed, making the offspring hatch on different days.

Two broods are often raised in a season and sometimes in the same cavity. Sometimes, additional chips are chiseled to cover the first nest before a second one is used.

Because the red-headed woodpecker is a great insect eater, it is a much desired species, both to farmer and city dweller. Almost half of its food is animal matter and half is vegetable matter. Ornithologists in examining stomach contents have noted the following insects to have been eaten: wasps, beetles, grasshoppers, crickets, moths and caterpillars.

The red-headed woodpecker has a long barbed tongue, three inches or more in length, that it extends into insect borer holes to spear the borer or grub and pull it from the tree fastened to the tongue. This trait is true of other woodpeckers as well.

Its vegetable diet included: corn, dogwood berries, strawberries, blackberries, raspberries, mulberries, elderberries, wild cherries, wild grapes, apples, pears, acorns, beechnuts, persimmons and varied seeds.

It stores food for winter use also. Acorns and various nuts have been stored in all sorts of places, such as cavities in trees, knot holes, cracks, crevices, bark seams, between shingles, and almost any type of opening it can find.

Some describe its cannibalistic habits as making it undesirable, for it has been known to enter bird houses and destroy eggs and young of other birds as well as eat all kinds of fruits from the orchards. However, the harmful insects that it destroys will more than make up for this aspect of its life.

Commonly referred to as "redhead", it is known as "Mr. redhead", just "red", or sometimes "white-wing".

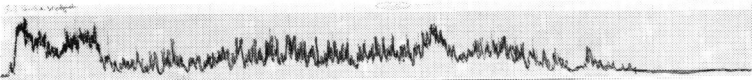

RED-HEADED WOODPECKER

20.

YELLOW-SHAFTED FLICKER*
(Coláptes aurátus)
length - 13 to 14 inches

Man's spring awakening could be due to the ringing call, a loud "wicker, wicker, wicker" sound across the area, the call of the flicker, so named because it is echoic of its note.

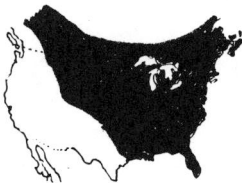

One of the most enjoyable sights of early spring is to see the mating dance of two males around a small diametered sapling attempting to attract a female, or, to hear two ardent suitors drum their courting messages on dead limbs of tree trunks, the gutter, downspout, television antenna, or whatever other resonant piece is available. Often this is early in the morning before the sun rises, much to the annoyance of some people but appreciated by all who love birds. There is perhaps no other bird that can furnish a more enjoyable courtship exhibition.

The flicker's flight in up and down rhythm clearly marks this bird. Its size also helps identification.

Its range for winter and summer residence is primarily east of the Rockies but it may winter west of this mountain range.

*Now named Common Flicker by A.O.U.

Its plumage resembles the red-shafted woodpecker of the west except for yellow shafts of wing and tail feathers instead of red. With a head of gray, cheeks and throat of brown, it has an identifying black crescent on its breast and a conspicuous white rump patch, quite noticeable as it flies up from the ground. The male has a black moustache and both sexes wear a red crescent on the nape. The golden yellow under-surface is quite visible, too, in its cross-country flight.

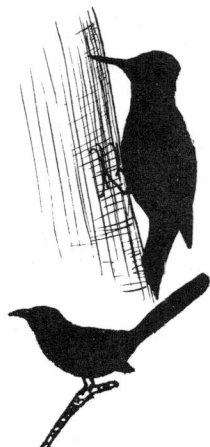

It prefers an open country near large trees, open pine barrens, or the edge of swamps, particularly if they have suitable nesting sites. It can be found in open woods, farm lands, and suburbs of our cities also. This bird has provided more nesting places for other birds than perhaps is true of other species, from its abandoned holes and cavities from year to year. Its similar calls of "yuker, yuker, yuker" and "wick, wick, wick, wick" help to identify this favorite of ours.

Its wintering desires to be indoors, particularly inside of the shutters of closed windows, has caused many humans great despair in their struggles to discourage house destruction.

This woodpecker will accept a bird box, particularly when dead trees are not available in which to carve out a cavity for nesting. The box should be approximately eight by eight inches and fifteen to twenty inches deep with a two and one-half to three inch entrance hole placed near the top of the box. The house location may vary from eight to fifty feet above the ground level and should resemble the dead tree as much as one can manage, probably erected against such an existing tree. If such a tree is not available, try placing the house on a large oak that is beside a creek or pond, facing parallel to the shore line or toward the water. A lone dead tree in an open field is a good location also.

The flicker house can also be placed atop a pole about ten feet high with a squirrel guard beneath the house. Make the pole and house as natural looking as possible. The flicker is not an easy bird to attract to a house but as soon as it finds a house that it likes, it is likely to return year after year.

5-10
glossy white, unmarked
1.1 in. x .9 in.

The nest of the flicker is made of chips of wood, sometimes with small amounts of sticks.

It incubates its eggs in a period of fourteen to sixteen days, with the young remaining another thirty days before flight. Both sexes join in digging out the nest chamber and both feed the young.

The flicker is a prolific egg layer. Often as many as thirty or forty eggs have been laid over three or four periods due to the destruction by other birds or by squirrels. It raises only one brood a year.

It is a prolific ant eater, often seen on an ant hill devouring a great quantity, as many as four or five thousand ants. Its food consists of about 50% animal matter, 20% insects and 30% vegetable matter. Besides ants it also eats beetles and grubs of various insects from lawns and tree trunks.

Its vegetable diet consists of bayberries, seaweed parts, berries, and other weed seeds. It sometimes devours wild fruits of various kinds.

Frequently seen at the suet feeder in winter, it will also

partake of other bird seeds if they are nearby.

It is often referred to as "yarrup", "yellow hammer", "pigeon woodpecker", "wake-up", "Harrywicket", "gaffer woodpecker", "high-hole", "golden-winged woodpecker" but most often just "flicker".

PHOTO BY DAVID G. ALLEN

YELLOW-SHAFTED FLICKER

111

21.

EASTERN PHOEBE
(Sayórnis phoébe)
length — 6¼ to 7¼ inches

Little phoebe is a favorite of all who are fortunate enough to have this little fly-catcher nest in their area. It gets its name from its call, a pleasant song, "fee-bee", "fee-bee", clearly sounding its name wherever it goes. An early spring arrival, it is a welcomed sight to farmers as well as city dwellers, for its insect eradication assistance and its pleasant habits. It arrives in full song, flitting about, snatching insects on the wing, particularly termites as they swarm.

The phoebe has no distinct field markings but is easily found by its up and down twitching tail. It has been described by some as reserved, graceful and swift. It is a bird that remains for a longer season than most species, six months being a usual stay. This is another reason for man to attract this bird if he can.

Originally the phoebes nested on rocky cliffs, in ravines and along all types of streams where water was nearby. Today, though, they have chosen the farmer's barn or yard and the city dweller's habitat. They have quickly adapted to man-made houses and have no particular preference except for size, preferring a smaller house.

It is often referred to as the bridge peewee because of its love for building among the underpinnings of bridges.

Since the phoebe likes a shelf to build upon, one placed under the eaves of a house, against the wall of a garage, barn, or storage house, and placed from eight to twelve feet above the ground will serve quite well.

A small bird house will also attract the phoebe, especially if placed in one of the locations just described, but perhaps not as likely as the open shelf.

The phoebe builds its nest of a variety of materials. Their nests have been found to contain green moss, mud, dry grass, grapevine fibers, feathers and animal hair. The nest is small in size, usually round and about four and one-half inches in diameter. The inner cup of the nest is only about two and one-half inches across. Nest building takes about thirteen days but sometimes less time is taken to complete the job. The phoebe sometimes repairs the nest for a second or third breeding period, though it is more likely to build again to avoid parasites that sometimes overrun the nest, only occasionally superimposing the second nest upon the original one.

The average incubation period is about sixteen days, with the female alone performing the task. Both parents, however, feed the young. Another sixteen to eighteen days is required for the young to reach near-adult size before leaving the nest.

The postnuptial molt takes place about August or September with the young taking on full adult plumage before fall and winter migration.

The juvenile plumage resembles that of the adult, but

the upper parts are browner. When full adulthood comes, the bird takes on a more olive or gray-brown color above and yellowish brown to buffy-white below, with a dark black bill and absence of wingbars which are prominent while juvenile. The phoebe also has black feet, legs and eyes.

3-8, 5 common;
white, sometimes
spotted
.8 in. x .6 in.

The phoebe is an insect eater almost entirely, with about 90% of its diet being animal matter. The animal matter consists of beetles, cotton-boll weevils, sawfly larvae, leafhoppers, grasshoppers, crickets, ticks, millipedes, and small dragonflies. The other vegetable matter, about 10%, is made up of small wild berries and seeds. The vegetable matter seems to be taken in the fall, winter or early spring, when insect life is dormant and not readily available.

The phoebe is often referred to as "barn pee-wee", "bridge pee-wee", "phoebe bird", "tick bird", and "pewit".

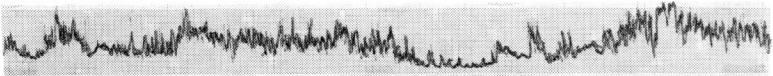

EASTERN PHOEBE

22.

(AMERICAN) ROBIN*
(Túrdus migratórius)
length - 9 to 10¾ inches

The American robin is not a robin but of the thrush family. Our English forefathers called him robin after their well known robin redbreast of European literature and folklore. Their robin was a much smaller bird, though, but similar in general coloration. Robin is a diminutive of Robert, of old High German origin denoting "glory, fame, bright."

Our robin is among our best known birds. It is commonly seen throughout the United States on lawns searching for insects and earthworms and particularly on highway grass plots as we drive along. Beautifully portrayed in its brick-red vest and charcoal-gray coat with black head, it is a sight to behold as it runs a few feet, opens its wings, and when finding a worm, braces itself as it struggles to pull the worm from its place. Often portrayed in paintings in just such a pose, this is realistic to those who have observed this bird in real life situations. It has a black streaked white throat and a dark tipped dusky-yellow bill, buffy-brown feet and legs and eyes set in a circular patch of light color.

*Now named American Robin by A.O.U.

The robin is our largest thrush. It is a very common winter visitor across the southland, and now has become a yearlong resident there. It is a migratory species, however, and many move northward in large flocks in springtime.

In Audubon's day robins were slaughtered by the thousands for their excellent eating. Today, however, the widespread use of insecticides is the great threat to this species. Their eating of earthworms that have eaten soil mixed with these harmful insecticides has caused the robins to eat fatal amounts of the pesticides.

Robins, like mockingbirds and cardinals, frequently attack their own images reflected in a windowpane, sometimes carrying this on day after day.

The robin prefers a shelf to build on instead of a house to build in. The shelf should be open on two or three sides and should be covered over. It should be placed from six to fifteen feet off the ground and on a limb or against the trunk of a tree, securely fastened. Man's provided shelf does not always attract the robin, for it just may build a nest nearby on a tree limb instead of the shelf that he has provided. Just the exact location for the robin's preference is not always easy to find. I have had a pair refuse my shelf offer and build nearby on a horizontal limb about fifteen feet off the ground and within a few feet of a yard swing that was used almost daily. This provided excellent entertainment throughout the summer months. This pair seemed to pay us little attention.

The robin builds a nest structure of coarse twigs tied together with pieces of string or cloth. Weed stalks and dry twigs are often found. A clay cup mixed with grasses to hold it together is built upon this coarse twig heap. The nest is about eight inches across with the inner cup measuring about three inches wide and one and one-half inches deep.

2-5, 3 common; greenish blue, rarely spotted

In early well forested days, the robin virtually built all its nests on horizontal limbs, in tree crotches or between the branches; but as man felled the trees countless additional sites had to be found. The robin rapidly became man's friend and neighbor, breeding freely in cities as well as countryside.

It can now be found nesting on window ledges, in rain pipes or gutters, under eaves, on fire escapes, on beams outside of buildings, porches and many other places.

The nest is built chiefly by the female with only occasional assistance by the male. The female always shapes the nest and performs most of the incubation.

The robin nest is kept scrupulously clean with the parents carrying away the fecal sacs.

Robins seem to have territories that they guard, though these areas are small. They seem usually to be apprehensive, restless, disturbed and upset by the least alarm, but this lasts only momentarily; otherwise, they are described as robust, confident and straight forward.

Incubation takes from eleven to fourteen days with the young remaining for another fourteen or fifteen days. Incubation is done mainly by the female, if not entirely. Two and possibly three broods are raised each year. They show persistency in their nesting habits, often returning to the same nest or location year after year.

Albinism is common in the robins, much more so than in other birds. When the young take on their first feathers, they show the spotted breasts of the thrush family. These spots and blackish streaks of the breast gradually change until about October when the adult plumage appears.

Close examination will reveal the young at this stage to have a duller and more muted color, somewhat browner with head less dark. This plumage remains until the second post-nuptial molt during the next August and September. The sexes look alike in the juvenile birds until complete adulthood, and then the females can be distinguished from the males by their duller colors, typical in the female bird species.

The robins food consists of about 60% vegetable matter and 40% animal matter. Among the vegetable matter items are fruits of the red cedar, greenbrier, mulberry, pokeweed, Juneberries, blackberries, wild cherries, sumac, woodbine, wild grapes, dogwood, blueberries, chinaberries, and many others of the local environment.

I have witnessed the robins love for ripe chinaberries in deep winter when a large number ate excessively of the ripe fruit that made them quite intoxicated, wobbling in the snow, unable to stay erect — just like humans look when they imbibe too freely. Recovery, however, with the robins was much more swift than with humans for they seemed to be able to fly away by evening.

Some people complain of the robins devouring their domestic fruit to a large extent. The good they do in insect eradication would seem to offset their unwanted fruit eating, though. One way to combat this has been offered as raising wild fruits that are in the diet of this bird, thereby distracting them from the orchard fruit.

Its alarm call is a "tut, tut" or "skut, skut" in a hissing manner but the robin's springtime call of "cheerily,

cheerily" heralds the beginning of another year.

The robin is sometimes referred to as "the American robin" and "Robin Redbreast."

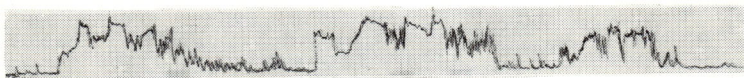

PHOTO BY ARTHUR A. ALLEN, CORNELL UNIV.

AMERICAN ROBIN

23.

STARLING
(Stúrnus vulgáris)
length - 8 inches

The word **starling** is from Old English **staerline** and Middle English **sterling** or **starling,** (**stare** plus **linc**) meaning "glitter" and also named for its cry.

It is considered to be an abundant pest across the country where it dwells in city parks, suburbs, farms, most anywhere. It is a gregarious bird and aggressive, so much so that it is often deadly to other birds. Its sharp, pointed bill permits it to thrust its bill into the head of an opponent with great ease, killing it almost instantly.

The starlings are especially abundant at roosting sites and it is not easily driven away by man. Their flocks have taken over many of our city buildings at eveningtime, when they roost together by the thousands. These large communal roosts are found from late summer until spring. Often these birds flock together with grackles and cowbirds to take over the winter bird feeders in a short time, if permitted to do so.

They can be distinguished from the cow bird and other blackbirds by their yellow bills (adult), for the starling is the only adult black bird that has a yellow bill. While still

in the immature or juvenile stage, however, the yellow bill is not established. It reveals itself then by its speckled white breast and darker brown to black wings. The short tail of the starling helps to separate it from the other blackbirds, along with its long bill. The feathers are a glassy blue, green, purple mixed with white, gray and yellow spots. Its legs are dark and feet robust. It has a wadling walk.

First introduced into the United States in the New York area around 1900, these birds now live in every state of the mainland United States as well as across southern Canada.

My own experience with the starlings is that it is easier to discourage them from the bird house then the house sparrows. I have been successful with the starling but not with the sparrow, particularly when discouraging the starling before nest building begins.

There seem to be only two simple, distinct migration routes that are used by starlings, northward in the spring and southward in the fall. All do not leave at either time, however, thus breaking a true migration pattern.

These birds are not very particular where they nest, nor do they seem to care about the condition of the nesting site. The nests are fouled during most of the period of nesting. They build over doors or windows, behind blinds, on ledges, in bird houses, in tree cavities, woodpecker holes, and wherever there seem to be vacant places.

We list the starling among the birds that build in man-made houses because they certainly do, and if you have been unsuccessful in attracting your favorite bird, then the starling perhaps can be accepted and will provide a season of enjoyment. The fight between the starling and the sparrow will provide entertainment indeed. Both may live side by side in a colony-type house.

The starling lays a beautiful egg, often of varying shades of blue, from a pale blue or greenish white to an almost white — all with a slight gloss.

The incubation period is eleven to fourteen days with both sexes sharing the responsibility. The young remain for a period of two to three weeks. The total cycle from nest building through flight time is about forty days. Two broods are usually raised each year and the same nest is used from year to year for several years. This untidyness and continued reuse makes the accumulation of rotted matter quite foul.

4-8
pale blue, unmarked
1.2 in. x .9 in.

The starling cannot enter bird boxes that have an entrance hole of one and one-half inches in diameter or less, so, if you do not prefer starlings, then you can eliminate them by using a small entrance hole and thereby keep the choice of birds to those that use the smaller holes.

Coarse grass fibers, fine grasses, straw, rootlets, twigs, corn husks, green leaves, bits of cloth, paper, string, feathers, and various trashy materials are used to make the nest. The size of the nest varies and the cup of the nest is about three inches in diameter.

The food of the starling consists of 57% to 60% animal matter and the remainder vegetable matter, depending upon availability. The clover leaf weevils and other weevils, ground beetles, May beetles, dung beetles, Japanese beetles, leaf beetles, potatoe beetles, spiders, snails, sowbugs, earthworms, beach flies, and many other insects make up its diet. The vegetable matter consists of cultivated and wild fruits and berries, with seeds mixed in. The starling's fondness for the weevils that feed on grass or forage crops has caused some to assert that "the starling is the most effective bird enemy of the clover beetles in America."

The starling has acquired fame as a mimic as it sounds the call of the bob-white, the killdeer, the flicker, the phoebe, wood peewee, chickadee, kinglet, yellow throat, house sparrow, bluebird, meadowlark, grackle, cowbird, goldfinch, and many other birds. Formerly it was caught and caged as a talking bird, for it can be taught various whistles and calls.

There are arguments pro and con about the starling and one must decide for himself whether he wishes a pair to nest in one of his bird houses.

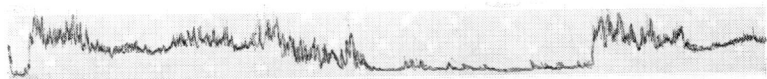

PHOTO BY DAVID G. ALLEN

STARLING

24.

GREAT CRESTED FLYCATCHER
(Myriárchus crinítus)
length - 8 to 9¼ inches

Perhaps at one time this large flycatcher frequented the woodlands but in recent years it has been found to dwell more and more in the cities and towns. Lightly wooded areas are now a choice of this species, for today it is seldom found in densely wooded areas.

Old apple orchards for this bird, too, become a likely domicile; but it also likes to encroach upon other bird houses, particularly that of a purple martin colony.

The author has experienced its snake skin antics on more than one occasion as this bird took over martin apartments by placing a snake skin half inside and half outside the apartments. There is nothing that will drive the purple martins away faster than to find a snake skin inside the house, for the martin is utterly afraid of snakes. Whether this action of the great crested flycatcher is meant to drive other birds away or not is now questioned by some who have found that the bird has substituted materials like cellophane or aluminum foil for snake skins. Perhaps the bird is merely modernizing. Regardless, my experience of sudden absenteeism of purple martins has on every occasion been the result of the snake skin placements. It is a bit uncanny just how this bird manages to find snake skins but it usually does, and this becomes part of the nest.

His reddish brown wings and tail, his yellowish green underparts and his smoke-gray crest seem to blend together well with the foliage that he likes to be in. It also has a light gray bill, dark gray feet and legs, and dark brown eyes. Away from trees and shrubs, his colors are a dead give away, however, as he sallies forth to catch an insect on the wing or to drive an intruder away. I have noted a characteristic of this bird to be his curious extending of his head suspiciously in different directions more than other species, particularly as he captures another bird's house — as if expressing a feeling of guilt. He is quite a fighter when he decides to build his nest and usually is the winner in most any struggle.

Its broad bill, large head, and insect catching habits help in the crested flycatcher's identification. It has many traits of the kingbird, especially its darting out and back in insect catching, but its stature is more erect, its tail longer, and its inclination to use the shade more will help in distinguishing this bird from the kingbird and from others.

Both male and female look alike in their plumage, and the young take on their full adult plumage before the first migration in late fall. The family seems to remain together after the young begin to fly and do so for some while.

The song of the flycatcher is a series of throaty whistling notes of "wheep" or rolling "preet", "wheep", or "queep", repeated.

Like many other species, this bird, too, will take over

abandoned woodpecker holes and other crevices of trees. It has no fear of man, however, and will use a wide variety of man-made houses, particularly if other birds seem to like them also. Boxes placed in similar locations as deserted woodpecker holes will serve a likely place to attract this bird. It has been known to build in a hollow log attached to a building, hollow posts, in old garden pumps, stove pipes, open gutters, old tin cans, and even shoe boxes.

4-8, 5 common;
creamy white,
brown streaked
.9 in. x .7 in.

It adapts its nest size to the chosen site, sometimes building a small nest and sometimes building a larger and deeper nest, depending upon the size of the cavity. The nest usually is found from six to eleven feet above the ground, and while not a colony bird, it will build in a colony box for martins that is erected at higher locations. It returns to the same site year after year in many cases. The nesting box should have a two inch diameter entrance hole and may be placed on the top of metal poles similar to bluebird house installations.

The nest is made of leaves of deciduous trees, and is mixed with animal hair, feathers, bark fibers, rootlets, pieces of string, strans of rope, cellophane, aluminum foil, snake skins, pine needles, cloth, paper, oil paper, seed pods, bits of egg shell, and many other items that are nearby.

The incubation period is between thirteen to fifteen days. The female tends to the incubation almost exclusively. Some have noted the female flycatchers to be somewhat careless setters, with addled eggs found on the nest quite often. This perhaps is due to their nervous instinct.

Both parents seem to tend the feeding duties until the

young are able to fly, which is another twelve to thirteen days. Food for the young consists of medium-small insects, with an occasional small butterfly included. A large percentage of larvae is fed also, accounting for approximately 25% of the food. Grasshoppers, spiders, moths, beetles, flies, bees, wasps, and other miscellaneous insects account, in large, for the remaining animal food.

About 6% of the diet is vegetable matter consisting of small wild fruits such as mulberries, raspberries, chokeberries, wild cherries, Virginia creeper, wild grapes, huckleberries, blueberries, and elderberries. The remaining 94% of the diet is animal matter, largely insects of the environment.

Most of the insects are taken on the wing but it has been noted that during the early part of the spring season, before the leaves appear, the flycatcher's food is taken near the ground or from the bark of trees and the crevices of fence rails and fence posts.

It is also referred to as "northern or southern crested flycatcher", "wheys", or sometimes "yellowhammer".

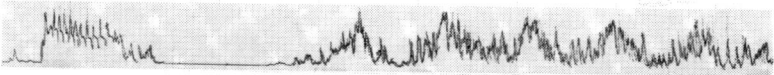

GREAT CRESTED FLYCATCHER

25.

BARN OWL
(Týto álba)
length - 15 to 21 inches

The American barn owl is widely distributed across North America southward from the lower Great Lakes region and is particularly abundant in lower California.

The owl gets its name from Middle English **owle**. The Latin words **ulula** owl, or **ululare** to howl, are echoic of the name as well as the later English words.

Owls have throughout history been associated with mystery and superstition, due to their nocturnal nature and especially so with the barn owl, for it frequents barns, empty houses, and other buildings often associated with stories about the "haunted house." Instead, it should be regarded as one of the finest of our feathered friends. It eradicates more than its just share of rodents that destroy the crops of man.

Its common note in flight is a widely spaced hissing tone. Other varied tones are sounded around the nest including screams, nighthawk-like calls, and snapping noises made by its bill.

It raises its family close to civilization and shows little fear of man though man is this owl's greatest enemy.

One owl can catch and feed its young as many as twenty-one mice each hour and consumes its own weight each day. Its catch is swallowed whole, head first, by adults and the young.

Ornithologists say that seventy to eighty acres of territory are needed to support one pair of these birds.

The barn owl is virtually noiseless in flight, with hearing so acute that it need not see its prey in order to pounce upon it.

As the falcon is often described as like a dive bomber, so can this barn owl be compared to a serveillance aircraft as it soars across the grassy meadows looking for field mice, shrews, frogs, and fish. It hovers like a helicopter when need be and turns its head from side to side in search of prey. This head turning of owls is necessary because they cannot turn thier eyeballs. Since it cannot turn its eyeballs, it turns its head, and seemingly in a 360 degree circle, but not so, just almost so. It must reverse its head eventually and turn back to the other way. Its three dimensional vision, however, permits it to have 100 times the light gathering capability of human beings.

Wind direction seems to have little effect upon this glider as it pursues its meal. Usually, it does not pounce upon its prey until the intended object has stopped momentarily.

The barn owl is easily recognized anywhere and at any time by its unique shape and color. Its general color is a tawny gray spotted with black and white above and white below. It has long legs that are completely feathered, including the feet. The nearly heart shaped face is a dead give-away when it perches. When in flight its buffy upper plumage, light or white underpinnings and long wings, light flight, hovering and reeling from side to side mark it distinctly.

Throughout most of its range from forests to fields, cliffs, semi-arid areas, cities and farms, it is a permanent resident.

The great horned owl seems to be its chief natural enemy, for the barn owl cannot fend against this larger, stronger adversary. Too, man still is an arch enemy, so often needlessly killing these birds because of their seeming destruction of game birds or poultry, or just to mount one, since it is such a beautiful bird.

3-12, 5-7 common;
white, unmarked
1.6 in. x 1.2 in.

Stomach contents have revealed this bird only occasionally to devour a game bird, or any birds. Its diet is principally mice, rats, shrews, moles, skunks, and young rabbits. Pocket gophers, destroyers of crops in the west, are among the favorite food of this owl. Insects such as grasshoppers, beetles, and katydids make up a part of its diet.

The barn owl coughs up the skeleton of its prey after digestion takes place and scientists have examined these pellet remains to determine this owl's eating habits. One such examination of two hundred remains revealed a total of four hundred and fifty-four skulls. Of these there were two hundred and twenty-five meadow mice, two pine mice, one hundred seventy-nine mice, twenty rats, six jumping mice, one mole, and one vesper sparrow. This hardly reveals the barn owl as a destroyer of birds.

The house for the barn owl should be about ten by eighteen inches deep. The entrance hole should be about six inches in diameter and it should be placed about four inches off the floor of the house. The house should be erected twelve to eighteen feet above the ground on a sill inside of a barn, garage (away from the house), boat house, or tool shed. Sometimes a location under the eave of these houses will entice the barn owl.

The male selects the site and once the female becomes a mate the two remain together for several seasons.

The plumage of the sexes is relatively alike. The female incubates the eggs most of the time with some assistance from her mate. He brings food for her to eat. The eggs hatch after twenty-four to thirty days and the young remain on the nest for seven to eight weeks longer.

The nest, when there is one, is inside of rubbish or debris. Usually there is no nest and the brooding area is not a neat, clean sight — anything but this. How the young manage to stay as clean as they do is somewhat of a mystery.

The barn owl is often called the "monkey-faced owl", the "white owl" and the "golden owl."

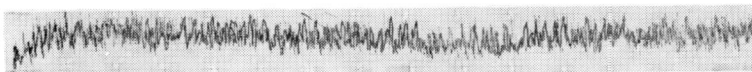

BARN OWL

26.

SCREECH OWL
(Ótus ásio)
length - 8 to 10 inches

This is our most common of owls. It is the small eared owl of both town and country.

A small owl, with yellow eyes and prominent eartufts is quite likely to be a screech owl. Named screech for its eerie, wailing cry, it seldom screeches. This small owl has a call described as more like a siren whistle, beginning with a low and full note gradually rising without the usual tremolo until it reaches a shrill shreik.

Thoreau, *while sitting on a stump by his door in Lincoln Woods listening to birds of the night, gave this graphic description of the screech owl:

It is no honest and blunt tu-whit tu-who of the poets, but, without jesting, a most solumn, graveyard ditty, the mutual consolations of suicide lovers remembering the pangs and the delights of supernal love in the infernal groves. Yet I love to hear their wailing, their doleful responses, trilled along the woodside; ...**Oh-o-o-o-o that I never had been bor-r-r-r-n!** sighs one on this side of the pond, and circles with the restlessness of despair to some new perch on the gray oaks. Then — **that I never had been bor-r-r-r-n!** echoes another on the farther side with tremulous

sincerety, and — **bor-r-r-r-n!** comes faintly from far
in the Lincoln woods.

The call of the screech owl is seldom heard until after
dark.

The newly hatched owls are white from tip of head to tip
of toe. The adult owl is a general mixture of gray and
brown colors with a grayer hue in the western part of the
United States and a darker brown hue in the eastern part.
There are several color phases of the screech owl. The
young go from the white phase through a gray phase with
streaked black plumage, black claws and black bill. Then
an adult phase of red, or rufous, above and white below
becomes evident.

It is seldom seen in the daylight hours unless found inac-
tive, dozing in some hollow tree, some dark corner, or hud-
dled up close to the trunk of some densely foliaged tree. I
shall always remember those two bright eyes on the limb
of a willow tree one night as we were
searching for beavers on the pond.
There, sitting alone, about twelve feet
off the ground was this little owl, quite
awake and alert to all that was trans-
piring below, for it was then about 9
p.m.

The hearing of the screech owl, as in
other owls, is quite acute. When found
during daylight hours in one of its
resting positions, paying little attention to the rustle of man, the little bird
may seem likely to be hard of hearing
with an inability to see during the day. Not so — he has

* Thoreau, Henry David, **Walden**, p. 113, New York: Random House, 1937

both seen and heard, just not caring. The screech owl is a gentle bird. Often it can be lifted from the nest or roosting hole or perch without much resistence, perhaps with a bit of bill snapping but seldom using its claws, thankfully, because they are sharp as needles. These owls have been said to make good pets but we do not recommend this for the owl's sake alone, if not for yours. The owl belongs in the out-of-doors.

This owl is our most likely man-made house acceptor among owls, but we suggest that you beware of its canibalistic traits, for it will catch and devour any small bird, preferring to reach into the nest at night to get a young bird, or adult even, or an egg or two. In a bird sanctuary it is an unwelcomed guest, for its stomach has been found to contain juncos and song sparrows, with a listing of other birds too long to mention.

The tremulous and lugubrious wailings of the screech owl during mating season in early spring mark its most active vocalization, which occurs during night hours, of course.

3-9, 4 common;
white, unmarked
1.4 in. x 1.3 in.

These birds will nest in bird boxes, set up in trees or on the sides of buildings. An eight by eight inch apartment with a ten to fourteen inch depth is preferred, with a three inch entrance hole near the top of the front side. The houses should be placed at a height above the ground of ten to thirty feet. A little sawdust, excelsior or wood shavings in the bottom will be quite to their liking.

One purple martin landlord found a screech owl nesting in one of the apartments of a purple martin colony, and even though an enemy of the martin, the owl raised its family side by side without harm to the martins. This is an unusual instance and the absence of cannibalizing the martins was due perhaps to the need of attention given to nesting of the owls. The owls left after their young could fly and the martins were said to have taken over their apartment immediately.

Usually the purple martin landlord's experiences have been of the detrimental behavior of the screech owl, which visits the colony at night to reach in and fly off with young or adult birds or eggs.

The period of incubation is reported as being from twenty-one to thirty days, with the average being about twenty-six days. Incubation begins when the first eggs are laid and continues until all the eggs are hatched. Apparently the female does the incubating and brooding of the young but the male is the provider for the family. Only one brood is raised each year.

From the time the first egg is laid until the young leave the nest is about eight weeks.

The food of the screech owl is quite a variable bill of fare, including almost every class of animal life. Stomach examinations showed mice, lizards, fish, crawfish, scorpions, earthworms, shrews, rats, bats, moles, flying squirrels, chipmunks, spiders, snails, many species of birds, beetles, cutworms, grasshoppers, locusts, crickets, cicadas, katydids, moths, caterpillars, and many other insects.

Although birds do not form so large a proportion of the screech owls food as mammals do, the list is long and suggests, as we have indicated before, that a careful analysis be made before making a decision to erect a screech owl house. If you live on a large tract of land with a body of water and woods away from the house, you may decide to provide a house in that location, but if you are attracting and feeding birds, then you may wish to pass this one by.

The screech owl is often referred to as "mottled owl", "red owl", "cat owl", and "shivering owl".

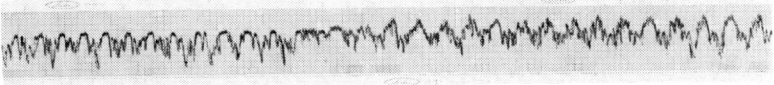

SCREECH OWL

27.

SAW-WHET OWL
(Aególius acádicus)
length - 7 to 8½ inches

This is one of the smallest owls, considerable smaller than the screech owl but considerably larger than the pygmy owl, differing from the screech owl in having a round head and no ear tufts. In complete adulthood it will measure about eight inches.

The saw-whet owl is a very tame owl, even to the extent that it is labeled stupid and fearless. It can be approached most easily, even within a few feet, often caught in the hand or under a hat or bag, when carefully approached.

It is essentially a bird of the woodlands, often found in the dark recesses of coniferous woods, preferring deep, shady, damp forests, near water. However, it has been found nesting in lawn trees close to the houses of people.

Known as the silent owl, it has a call in spring when its noisy raucous call is said to sound like the wheting of a saw — thus its name, saw-whet owl. It also has a series of whistled notes, closely spaced and sounded in rapid succession.

The nest of the saw-whet owl is usually fine chips. Sometimes it uses moss interwoven with small pieces of fibrous bark, a few pine needles, small twigs, and a few feathers.

The plumage of the saw-whet owl is beautiful. The upper parts are deep rich brown, "auburn" on the head and behind the neck, shaded off to a paler shade of the same color on the upper breast, with a darker brown on the back and wings. The head plumage has blotched brown streaks on the underparts mixed with white. The juvenile plumage is a lighter brown above and a more reddish brown on the under parts.

The first winter plumage is fully adult with the annual molt occurring between August and November.

Since the owl prefers to build its nest at low heights, less than twelve feet, it often selects old stumps to build in. Abandoned woodpecker holes, particularly flicker holes, are selected, though even at greater heights up to twenty feet or more. Since this is true, once can place the saw-whet owl's box in a similar location, perhaps on the side of a dead tree that has woodpecker holes at greater heights. Here, again, it is best to note the habitat of the owl before placing the house. You will be at a greater advantage if the house is near water and also near a wooded area; then the house will be more readily acepted by the species. Perhaps your flicker house will attract this owl, if you have not gotten a flicker or other bird already, and this owl may even move in if you have another bird already. Such is the way of this owl.

The house size should be about six by ten inches with a two and one-half inch entrance hole placed eight to ten inches from the floor of the house.

Incubation is estimated as being from twenty-one to twenty-eight days. The eggs are laid at intervals of from one to three days with incubation beginning with the first egg laying. This means an irregular hatching, resulting in the oldest bird being nearly ready to fly as the last egg is laid.

4-7, 5 or 6 common;
white, unmarked
1.3 in. x 1 in.

The young stay at the nest for another twenty-seven to thirty-four days before their first flight. Both sexes assist in incubation with the female doing the greater part as is typical of most species. Only one brood per year is raised.

The food of the saw-whet owl is made up of mice mainly, with some small rats, young red squirrels and flying squirrels, chipmunks, shrews, bats, and other small mammals comprising the remainder. A few birds have been found in the diet of this owl, but not to the extent of the screech owl. It is a silent night hunter, sleeping during the daytime in some evergreen thicket. It will eat twice its weight in one day, noted one observer. Though preferring small mammals it can kill birds and animals somewhat larger than itself.

It is seldom seen in high treetops, so if you are searching for this owl look among the lower branches. It dozes during the day at levels within a few feet of the ground.

Its common call is a series of three whistles, thus: "shreigh-au, shreigh-au, shreigh-au". The young make a hissing sound, usually common in the owl family.

The saw-whet owl prefers the northern section of the United States and across Canada for nesting but winters across middle America and into central Mexico. Sometimes it is seen in minor instances in other states as well.

This owl is also called "Acadian owl", "saw-filer", and "white-fronted owl."

SAW-WHET OWL

28.

SPARROW HAWK (KESTREL)*
(Fálco sparvérius)
length - 9 to 12 inches

The word **hawk**, Middle English **hauk**, meant to seize, take, or snatch — thus hawks were so named for seizing their prey on the wing.

This is the smallest and most common of the falcons in open and semi-open country. It has distinguishing marks of two whiskers on each side of its face and a rusty back. Many small hawks are called the sparrow hawk but on close observation they are not, for they do not carry these markings. A closer look at its plumage shows the sparrow hawk to have a rufous spot in the center of a blue-gray crown, a rufous back and upper tail. The back and upper side of the tail are more or less barred with a slight blackish hue; also there is a black streak under the eye to the throat area and a very similar streak running from the eye toward the rear of the head. The undersides vary from whitish to tawny with black spots along the flanks.

Its call is a shrill, rapidly repeated "killy-killy-killy-killy-killy".

The sparrow hawk is one of the few species in which the sexes are decidedly unlike in the juvenile plumage. The

*Now named American Kestrel by A.O.U.

color patterns of each sex are like its adult plumage — thus, making easy sex distinction at an early age.

The sparrow hawk will build in a man-made house, but it is not easily attracted. It is more likely to accept one in a rural setting than in a city or town setting. Occasionally it accepts an old nest of another bird and particularly the abandoned hole or box of the flicker. So, the flicker box is a likely place, or somewhere in its environs. It prefers a roofed over house instead of an open one. A square hole entrance will be accepted as well as a round one. The box should have approximately a nine by nine by twelve inch interior with entrance hole about two and one-half inches in diameter, placed near the top of the front side. These birds seem to like the boxes placed on single trees, those standing alone. Dead trees are good places upon which to place a house as are the outside walls of old buildings. An area where mice and grasshoppers are available offers an added attraction. Placing moth balls around the base of the pole or tree will deter predators from molesting the nest.

The sparrow hawk makes use of buildings as well as bird houses for its domicile. Sometimes it lays its eggs on the bare floor of the box or cavity, or accepts whatever the prior occupant left. Sometimes rotten bark and wood is used for the nest, if it makes a nest at all, and the nest will likely not be a neat one. An old pigeon box will be used sometimes by the sparrow hawk.

The incubation period is approximately thirty days and the young do not begin to fly for another thirty day period. Incubation is carried out by the female almost entirely.

Only one brood is raised each year.

The food of the sparrow hawk includes insects, small birds, mammals, reptiles, and amphibeans. Grasshoppers, when available, become a primary food. Crickets, mice, frogs, snakes, and some ants are also eaten.

4-5, 3 common;
creamy, yellowish, buff,
spotted, blotched
1.3 in. x 1.2 in.

Its lightness and switfness make it a favorite as it cruises along, soaring against the sky, wings stretched wide, ready to veer like a flash, to pounce upon its prey or to mount higher, to drop to the ground, or to come to rest on a little twig.

In fall these hawks migrate by the thousands to the new area, seemingly following the river streams.

In winter it is likely to be seen perched on dead stumps by the roadside or the side of an open field, on the wires along the road or railroad tracks, hovering over bare stubble in the field and nearly always alone.

In recent years it is seen more and more in the towns and cities, some have said because the house sparrows have moved there and they offer a better and easier diet to find. Birds, however, are seldom devoured as long as the regular diet of insects and mice is available. More and more it shows less fear of man, who is usually among its greatest enemies.

The sparrow hawk is sometimes referred to as "grasshopper hawk", "American kestrel", "killy hawk", "windhover", and "mouse hawk".

SPARROW HAWK (KESTREL)

151

29.

DOMESTIC PIGEON
(Colúmba lívia)
length - 11 to 13 inches

The word "pigeon" probably is an English corruption of the Italian word "piccione", which comes from the Latin word "pipi" or "pipire" meaning a bird that cooed or echoed its name.

The plumage of the pigeon is soft and thick with a variable color pattern that is mostly metallic or irridescent. Generally gray with purple tinge on its head, back and neck, it has a white rump area with broad terminal bar of black on the tail extremity. An irridescent green or bronze color is often found on the neck. It is a beautiful bird.

Dwelling in cities primarily, its roosting habits and prolific increase in population has made it undesirable in many areas. It is easily tamed and a show bird in European cities, especially the court yards and plazas. It has grown to be a bird dependent on man, its provider. The domestic pigeon can be seen circling in flocks across the city life, especially in the railroad yards where through generations it has learned to gather spilled grain and other edibles from railroad cars.

Feeding the pigeons in a city park is a common custom, much to the delight of the youngsters, whether at home or abroad and the pigeon is probably the one most familiar and recognizable of all birds, being the closest contact of many people with our world of birds.

Its familiar "coo-a-roo", "coo-a-roo", "coo-a-roo", "coo-a-roo" or just "coo, coo, coo" at daybreak is a familiar sound, wanted or unwanted, in downtown city life on its roosting or nesting ledge.

The pigeon is an excellent flier and a long-distance, rapid flier. Before days of radio, television or telegraph, many important messages were delivered by "carrier-pigeons" trained for this purpose. Cross-breeding of certain pigeons for flight purposes is quite a hobby now.

It is less frequently encountered in open country during winter but does frequent the farm buildings in summer.

It is a domestic bird that can be tamed easily. Also, it is raised by some for its edible qualities, the squab being a specialty when properly prepared by a fine chef. Piccioni in Salmi and Piccioni Arristo are excellent Italian dishes in the provinces of Toscana and Umbria, Italy.

This rock dove lives across the United States and is not generally a migratory bird.

This bird builds its nest on building ledges, cliff ledges, in boxes and in trees. Its nest is a rather untidy arrangement of sticks, twigs and grasses.

Normally one to three eggs are laid with two being common. Several broods are raised each year, overcoming its limited number of young that are raised each time.

Incubation takes seventeen to nineteen days and is carried out by both sexes. The young remain on the nest for

1-3, 2 common;
white, unmarked
1.5 in. x 1.1 in.

about thirty-five days before their first flight is undertaken.

Their food is largely vegetable matter. Various seeds and grains are eaten but it will scrounge for garbage remains in city and town. Animal matter includes insects, spiders and garbage remains.

If you are interested in raising pigeons, prepare a colony house for them. An enlarged purple martin type house can be placed atop the garage, garden house or similar structure, for the weight of the house usually is too much to erect atop a separate pole, at least it is more easily erected atop the already existing buildings. This location makes it accessible for cleaning too.

These birds are believed to mate for life, only remating when one of the pair dies. The affection of the mated pair and their solicitude and loving care with which they tend their young has been cited as exemplary to man and have secured an established place in literature and become a symbol of peace.

The pigeon fancier has a wide choice of varieties to choose from. While most pet stores do not stock pigeons, usually they can direct one to an individual pigeon hobbyist nearby. In choosing a pair, be sure to select a banded bird. This will insure proper information about the birds, particularly the age.

Proper raising of pigeons requires time, patience and effort. They must be fed properly with non-fibrous grain, grit and occasionally greens. Usually a reputable feed dealer can supply the foods needed. It is estimated that a large adult pair of pigeons will consume approximately one hundred pounds of grain during one year.

The coop must be kept clean, whitewashed periodically with a mixture containing a teaspoon of carbolic acid to the pail to assist in insect control. An open draining pan kept full of water for bathing will add to the pigeon's delight and cleanliness. Providing nesting materials such as straw, feathers and weed stems will prove helpful also. Then you should provide for protection against predators. Constant examination of the pigeon coop for mice, red mites, and lice is advised.

Pigeons become attracted to man and offer good pets, but one must decide before entering upon pigeon raising whether he has the time and willingness to support his birds before making the decision.

Common names are just "pigeon", "rock dove," "street pigeon", and "city dove".

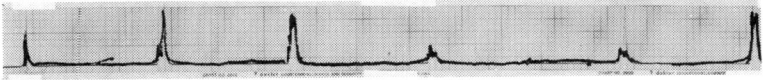

DOMESTIC PIGEON

30.

WOOD DUCK
(Aix spónsa)
length - 17 to 20 inches

Perhaps named **duck** because of its swimming, ducking antics, the word in Middle English was **doke**, Old English **duce** — both meaning diver or ducker. The descriptive adjective **wood** was given to this duck for its ability to fly through the woods, not a trait of other ducks, and its nesting in trees.

This is perhaps our most beautiful duck, the duck of the open woodlands along ponds, lakes and streams. The wood duck is strictly a North American species and principally a bird of the United States, extending only slightly into Canada.

It is one of the most widely distributed species, since it winters over much of its habitat in the United States.

To some it is known as "summer duck", to others "tree duck" from its habit of nesting in tree cavities.

Both sexes look very much alike except for the more brilliant wing pattern and different head pattern. No duck is so expert as the wood duck in threading its way through the tree branches, often compared to the dove in flight. It is a swift and agile swimmer and can dive at will, whether to escape or for food. Its call often sounded during flight, is a squealing "hoo-eek, hoo-eek", or a "jeeee" with rising tones.

The crown of both sexes is a clove brown or cinnamon shade but the male has a greenish luster. The female has a more noticeable white area around the eye, while both sexes have a duller gray pattern on the sides of the head and a white throat, the white of the male extending up to the neck. There is an irridescent gray background on the drake's beak. The bill of the drake is a variegated pattern of red, black and white. Both male and female are large crested and have chunky bodies.

These ducks select nesting sites with no seeming preference as to kind of trees or location, provided the tree has a large enough hole for it to enter and sufficient cavity in which to build. It, surprisingly, has been known to get through a flicker hole, perhaps enlarged, though preferring a larger entrance if it can be found. No particular effort is made to build a nest except for splinters of wood from the cavity walls and down and feathers from its own body. The size and depth of the cavity can vary widely as can the location. It prefers, however, trees that are near water but is known to build in houses that are placed near the water and also some distance from the water's edge.

The height of the nest varies from three to four feet to as much as fifty feet off the ground. This depends upon what the duck can find to build its nest in.

The wood duck returns to the same site for several years. Only one brood is raised each year.

Population of the wood duck is increasing, particularly in the south, due to man's efforts to provide nesting boxes to which it adapts.

10-15, 6-8 common; dull white, unmarked 2 in. x 1.6 in.

The incubation period lasts from twenty-eight to thirty days and is done completely by the female. The male is in attendance on his mate during the period and helps to care for the young. The young are born with sharp claws which they use in climbing from the nest cavity. The young drop from the cavity to the ground and are taken by the mother to the water. Sometimes they ride on her back to the water or follow in a group together. Even from heights the little ducklings do not often seem to get hurt in the jump to the ground. Once in the water the adults teach them to obtain their own food — insects, flies, mosquitoes, and seeds. As they grow up they eat dragon flies, grasshoppers, locusts, and aquatic life that includes small fish, minnows, frogs, tadpoles, snails, and small salamanders. Bulbs of root plants as well as seeds and plant leaves become a part of the diet. Food from wild rice marshes and from planted rice areas is readily accepted. Fruits and berries of the dry land are also eaten. Acorns, chestnuts, beechnuts, and water chinquapins are among its diet. About 90% of the wood duck's diet is made up of vegetable matter, the remaining 10% being animal matter.

The wood duck has always been able to hold its own against its natural enemies but has lost territory at the hands of man as he clears more and more of the wooded areas used for nesting. The wood duck is so tame that it is easily shot in large numbers and since it is a popular game bird, many are killed each year. The population now is controlled to a much better degree by hunting laws and seasons established and patrolled by wildlife protection agencies. This is good, both for the duck and for man's sake.

The wood duck is also called "summer duck", "wood widgeon", "acorn duck", and "tree duck".

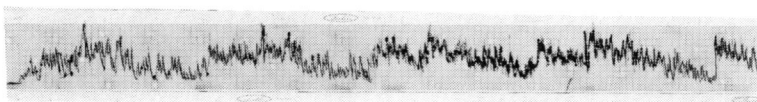

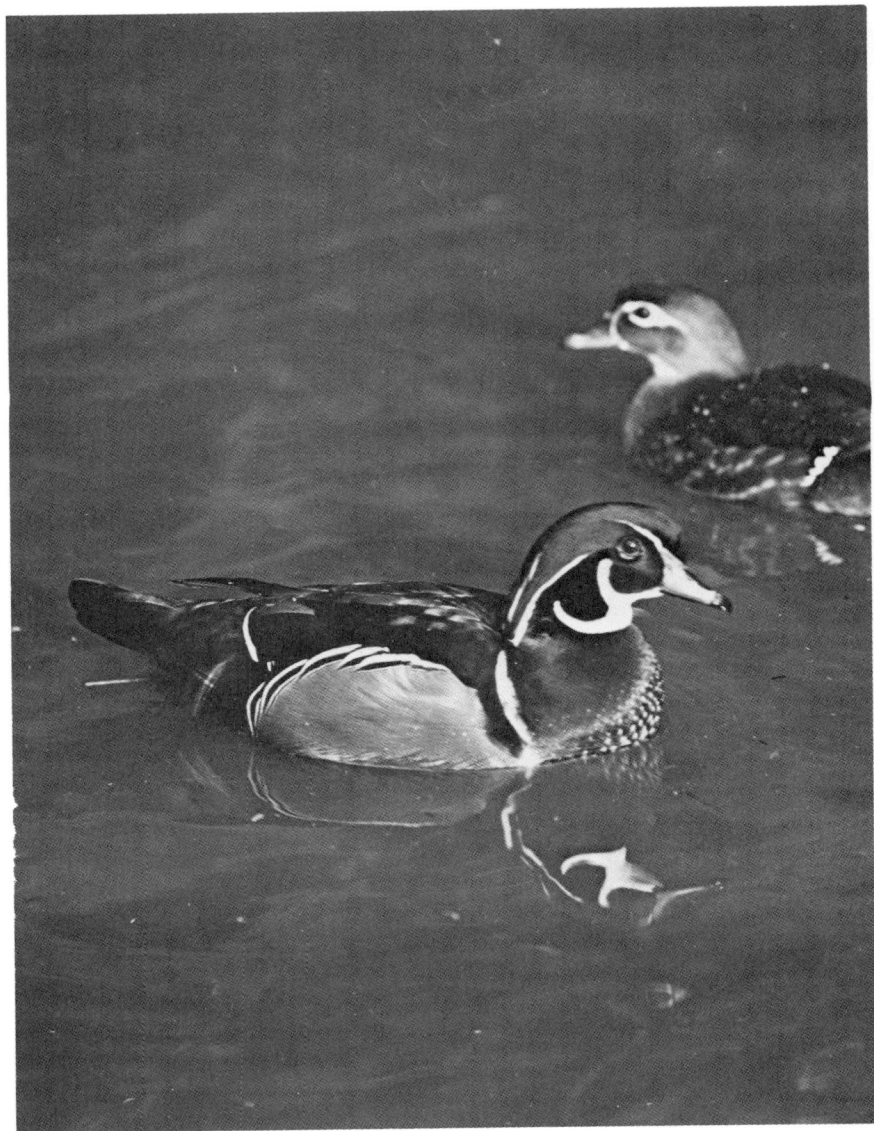

PHOTO BY DAVID G. ALLEN

WOOD DUCK

HOUSE PLANS

HOUSE PLAN NUMBER 1

This house is made of a cross-section piece of log or limb, about six to eight inches in diameter and about ten inches long. From the section, first cut off two slices about one-half to three-fourths inches thick. These will be nailed back again for the top and the bottom of the house, after you have cut the remaining cylinder into halves and cored the two pieces to leave two half-shells with about a three-fourths inch thickness ( ). Cut an entrance hole through one of the shell pieces about two inches from the end of the cylinder. Then attach the two half cylinders together. If you plan to attach the house to a tree, post, or pole, nail a one-inch by twelve-inch piece to the half cylinder before attaching the two half-cylinders together and before you cut the entrance hole. Then you can attach the house by nailing through the vertical piece both above and below the house ( ). By adding bark slivers or slices to the top and bottom, a more natural appearance will be had.

For: wrens, chickadees, titmice, warblers and other small birds.

HOUSE PLAN NUMBER 2

A favorite of the wrens, titmice, and chickadees is this popular, easily made house. Cut two pieces four inches by four inches for the ends and then cut two other pieces for the sides to be four inches by three and one-half inches (if using one-half inch thick pieces). Nail the two sides together, nailing through the edges of the four-inch piece into the edges of the three-and one-half inch pieces, then attach the back and the front. Drill the entrance hole through the front as shown and add a 2" long piece of dowel rod of one-fourth inch diameter for a perch. Attach the dowel rod through a quarter-inch hole that you have drilled at the appropriate place. Now nail the two top pieces on, being sure that the back edges are flush with the back of the house, not extending out as they do in the front. This little house may be placed at the most attractive area for your favorite wrens, either hanging, surface attached, or placed on top of a shelf or cabinet. Two 45° angle widges (◣ ◿) will need to be attached to the bottom sides for shelf or cabinet location. Pine cone scales may be attached as shown for added attraction. Use a staple gun to brad them on.

For: wrens, titmice, chicadees, warblers, and other small birds.

HOUSE PLAN NUMBER 3

This unique small bird house is made to be a part of an existing tree limb. The chosen limb from an existing tree is first cut off as shown and the branches removed from the remaining limb as shown in the drawing, except for a couple of twigs that may be left extending from the remaining stub. First, determine just the place for the entrance hole and mark it. Then cut across the limb at a right angle just above the entrance hole and cut a second time across the remaining part about six or eight inches below the entrance hole mark. This section that you have carefully cut out is then cored with a chisel, leaving an outer shell about three-fourths inches thick. Now cut the entrance hole at the marked place. By using nails attach the cored section back in place between the remaining tree stub and the outer end that you cut off. The completed house will then have the appearance of that in the drawing and will become a house for small birds.

For: wrens, titmice, chickadees, nuthatches, small woodpeckers and other small birds.

HOUSE PLAN NUMBER 4

Cut an eight inch diameter section of oak log, or other hardwood, about eight inches long. Then cut a cross-section off of one end about three-fourths inches thick. Use this for the bottom after you have cut out the core of the remaining cylinder. Next, cut across one end of the cylinder at a sloping angle (about 25°). Then cut the top eight inches by ten inches and the back piece eight inches by twelve inches. These are from one-fourth inch exterior plywood or one-half inch cypress or western cedar. Then attach the cylinder to the back piece with nails. The cored cylinder may be cut into two halves before coring and entrance hole cutting, which will permit easier attachment to the tree, post, or wall. Attach the top with hinges so the house can be cleaned out easily. Be sure that the same amount of overhang is on both sides before attaching hinges to the back board. Cut an entrance hole about one and one-half inches from the top front edge. Attach the house to a tree, fence, post, or wall.

For: wrens, titmice, chickadees, warblers and other small birds.

HOUSE PLAN NUMBER 5

The natural gourd offers an excellent house for not only purple martins but for many other species of birds as well, when clustered appropriately or used as single houses. The gourd is prepared by cutting an entrance hole at an appropriate place as shown and the size of the gourd will suggest the proper size hole to cut for the bird that will use that size gourd. The gourd/s can be located in the same places that you would locate other houses for the species. Particularly is this true for the wrens, who love gourds for their houses. Also, the gourds may be kept in their natural color or may be painted in various hues to suit the environment. The gourds can be hung from their necks by using cords, ropes, or wires that are laced through holes cut through the top of the gourd neck, thereby permitting it to swing. It may also be secured on a shelf or cabinet. Place it in your preferred spot. There are many sizes and many shapes of gourds to choose from, ranging from the small ornamental (for wrens), to the bushel size gourds (for large birds). Consult your farm journal or paper for a listing of seeds available for the planting of your own gourds if you prefer.

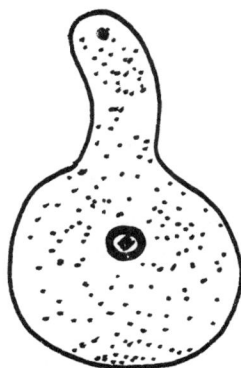

For: wrens, chickadees, titmice, house finches, warblers, purple martins and other birds.

HOUSE PLAN NUMBER 6

This is a decorative hanging type or attachment house for small birds. It shows the perch made by cutting two upright pieces drilled with a one-fourth inch diameter drill for an inserted limb, cane or dowel rod for a perch. The sides may be moss covered, pine scale covered, or twig bradded, if a more natural appearance is desired. This house may be hung from a limb, nailed to the side of a building, tree, fence or pole — or attached to the top of a fence post or pole. The dimensions are: front and back made of a piece with three inch bottom edge, five inch side edges, and four inch top edges; two sides with five inch bottom edges and five inch side edges; two top pieces with six inch side widths and five inches from peak to outside edge (one inch overhang included); bottom piece three inches by five inches. Begin assembling by attaching the side peices inside of the end pieces, then the bottom piece and then the two roof pieces. The edges may be attractively decorated with twigs that are nailed on. Cut the entrance hole as shown.

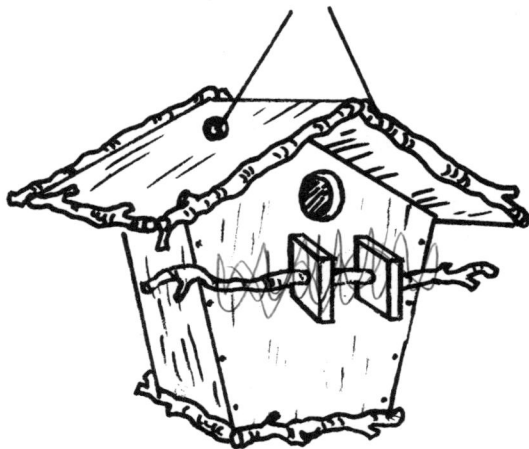

For: wrens, chickadees, titmice, warblers, swallows, and other small birds.

HOUSE PLAN NUMBER 7

This little Ethiopian hut may be hung from a favorite spot, attached to a tree, post, or side of a building. To construct it cut out four trapezoidal pieces with bases four inches and six inches, height two and one-half inches from your favorite building materials. These are the roofing pieces. Then cut out four other trapezoidal sides for the base sides, with bases four inches and five inches from a piece of material four inches by twenty inches (▽△▽△). Attach these four pieces together with the four inch sides at the bottom. By letting the four pieces overlap consecutively as you attach one piece on the other, the open area will be square (▢). Now nail the four roof trapezoidal pieces together in a similar fashion. These also will form a square opening. Cut the entrance hole through one of the sides as shown about one inch from the top edge. Next cut out the roof cover by using for a pattern the already attached four trapezoidal pieces that you have made for the top. Do the same for the bottom cover piece. Then attach these top and bottom square pieces, using nails or screws.

For: tree swallows, violet-green swallows, titmice, chickadees, warblers, as well as for other small birds.

HOUSE PLAN NUMBER 8

This shelf design may be made with these basic pieces: bottom, back, top, and two auxiliary pieces (side top brace and side bottom brace). The bottom is seven inches by nine inches, the back is nine inches by nine inches, and the top is eleven inches by eleven inches. The auxiliary pieces may be added, using your own dimensions for these, as well as your own pattern. Cut the top edge of the back at a slight angle (⌐) to tilt the roof forward. Attach the bottom to the back first, then the roof and lastly the two auxiliary pieces. These auxiliary pieces can be designed to fit flush with the back of just inside. Either will suffice. Brad pine cone scales on the roof for added attraction. Use a stapling gun for this. The completed house shelf should be located at an appropriate place to attract your favorite nesting bird.

For: robins, phoebes, barn swallows and tree swallows.

HOUSE PLAN NUMBER 9

To make this attractive house, cut an eight inch long cross-section from a tree or log. By choosing a section with limbs as shown in the drawing, one of these can be used for the perch later and the others as decorative pieces as shown. Now cut a three-fourths inch slice off the bottom of the cross-section, later to be used as the bottom of the house. You are now ready to cut across the top end of the cross-section at a desired slope — you be the judge. We suggest about 20° to 25° angle. Now use either one of two methods to remove the core from the cross-section. You may drill a one-inch hole through the section vertically at the center point and use a chisel to cut off pieces until a shell remains, or you may cut the cross-section into two halves ( ) and chisel out the core from each half, then nail the two halves together. Next cut an entrance hole at the position shown. Be sure that it is over the limb stub that you plan to use for a perch. The top, a piece ten inches by ten inches, is then nailed on, leaving the same amount of overhang on all sides; then nail on the bottom slice. Use screws instead of nails if you prefer.

For: wrens, chickadees, titmice, warblers, house finches, small woodpeckers and other small birds.

HOUSE PLAN NUMBER 10

This phoebe shelf if simple to make, since it only requires two boards, one vertical piece for the upright and one horizontal piece for the shelf. Since phoebes like to build under bridges, under porches, on accessible floor joists, on steel beams of bridges, and the like, a simple shelf is easy to make and locate. The plan shown is made of a one-inch by twelve inch by twenty-four inch board with a one inch by six inch by twelve inch center piece. Attach three small right angle braces as shown. Two braces may be sufficient. These braces are attached with metal screws or stove bolts to the under side of the existing structure. The underpinnings of a high elevation lodge or summer house will present a good location, too. The shelf may also be placed under the eave of a house, against the wall or other favorite location for this species.

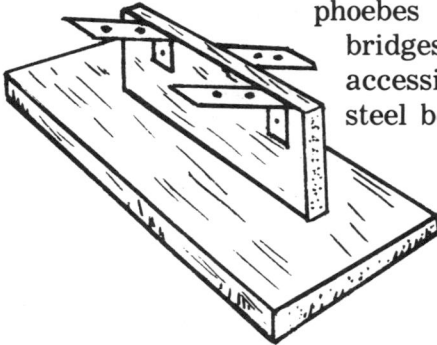

For: phoebes and swallows.

HOUSE PLAN NUMBER 11

This house is made of a tree cross-section about six inches in diameter and eleven or twelve inches long. First, cut off two cross-sections about three-fourths inches thick from the end of the chlindrical section. These are for the two ends. Next cut the remainder of the cylinder into two halves (). Then, using a chisel, cut out the core of each half cross-section, leaving a shell about three-fourths of an inch thick. Next, cut the front slice to fit into the shell (fig. 2) and attach it to the bottom half about two inches inside to permit an overhang for the roof and the porch. The entrance hole is then cut through

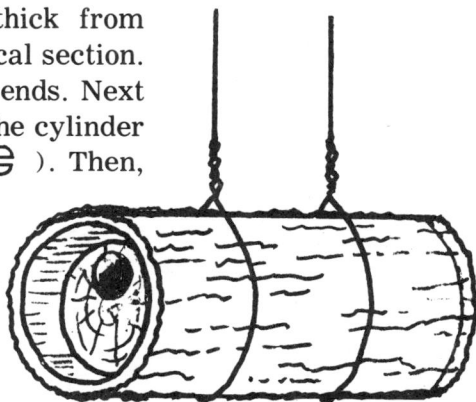

1   2

the upper part of the front end piece as shown. The two halves are held together by lacing two wires around the two half-cylinders as shown. The finished house will have a front roof overhang after the front and back ends are nailed on the lower half of the cylinder. You may need to drill small holes through the back end piece to prevent splitting the wood.

For: wrens, titmice, chickadees, small woodpeckers, warblers, nuthatches, and other small birds.

HOUSE PLAN NUMBER 12

This is a four-side-open shelf for mounting appropriately for a phoebe, robin, or song sparrow. The shelf is eight inches by ten inches by one-half inch. The four posts are made of cross-section tree limbs about one inch in diameter and about eight inches long. The roof pieces should be cut seven inches by ten inches and seven and one-half inches by ten inches. Attach the two roof pieces at 90° angle by nailing through the edge of the seven and one-half inch piece into the seven inch side of the other piece. Cut two triangular end roof gables to serve as braces for the roof. To assemble, attach the posts to the bottom piece at the four corners. Next, attach the roof to the four posts by nailing through the roof at an angle to make the nail or screw go perpindicularly into the posts. Attach the two gables under the roof ends as shown. Use bark slab boards to cover the roof, or bark slivers that you have cut from tree sections or fire wood pieces. The natural appearance will assist in attracting the birds that you have selected.

For: robins, phoebes, and song sparrows and some swallows.

HOUSE PLAN NUMBER 13

This popular flicker house is rectangular in shape with a sloping roof. Cut the following boards from one-half inch stock: two side pieces five and one-half inches by twenty inches and two other side pieces five and one half inches by eighteen inches. The two twenty inch pieces are sloped alike by placing one on top of the other and cutting the roof slopes off one end. This is determined by drawing from the center top edge to points on each side edge that are two inches below the top ( ). After sawing, the end design should have this shape ( ). Then assemble in the following manner. Attach the sides in consecutive order ( ), being sure that the front and back are opposite each other. This will leave a five inch square opening at bottom and top. Then cut a piece six inches by six inches for the bottom and nail it into place. Cut two pieces for the roof, nine inches by nine inches and attach them so that the back edge is even with the back side and the front and side edges overhang. This permits the house to be attached against the side of a tree, post, or wall. A security piece two inches by twenty-four inches may be nailed vertically across the house for attaching to the selected place. Then attach pine cone scales for added attraction to the roof and bark slabs to the sides, if desired. The completed house may then be erected in your selected spot.

For: flickers, downy and hairy woodpeckers, yellow-fronted woodpeckers, saw-whet owls and other small birds.

HOUSE PLAN NUMBER 14

This is another open shelf type and can be constructed easily. Basic dimensions are: back piece eight inches by fourteen inches, base eight inches by eight inches, top eight inches by ten inches, and side ten inches by ten inches (approximately). Make your own pattern for this side piece. It can be of two triangular pieces as shown or one piece by not cutting the open area all the way through ($\triangleright$). The top end should be cut at an angle to permit the roof to slope forward ($\triangleleft$).

The bracing upright side piece/s leaves the side partially open and still serves as a brace for the roof. The piece is attached with even edges, not projected, as shown, or projected to cover the back, top, and bottom edges. The triangular corners may be cut from the back as shown or the corners may be left at right angles, depending upon your preference. Bark or moss may be added for a more natural appearance.

For: robins, phoebes, and barn swallows.

HOUSE PLAN NUMBER 15

This vertical house for small birds was suggested by a section of willow tree that was cut by beavers and found floating in the lake. It resulted from a beaver second cut about a foot higher and had not been denuded of bark because the beavers did not choose to use it for their intended purpose. I sawed it lengthwise into two equal pieces, keeping the ends just as they were cut by the beavers, then cored an interior from each half to provide a cavity about six inches by nine inches. Then an entrance hole was cut in the middle top part of the front half, the back half being nailed to a tree in an appropriate place. Next, the front half was attached to the back half with aluminum nails. That year it was accepted by titmice. This same type of house is also attractive to other small birds and can be made with or without a perch and from a stick of oak or hickory fire wood of adequate diameter. The end designs can be cut to suit your taste in the event you have no beavers to assist you with this task.

For: small woodpeckers, wrens, chickadees, tree swallows, titmice, nuthatches, and other small birds.

HOUSE PLAN NUMBER 16

Construction procedures for this house for small birds are as follows. Cut two sides three inches by five inches by five inches with sloping top edge as shown (◁), then cut the front piece five inches by five inches, the bottom piece five inches by four inches, and the top piece seven inches by nine inches. A security piece, two inches by fifteen inches, may be used to attach the completed house to a pole, post, tree, or wall — or, you may suspend it from a limb without this piece. Begin by nailing the front piece to the two side pieces. Then attach the back piece in a similar manner, then the bottom piece and finally the top piece. Be sure that the top is flush with the back of the house, evenly extending as roof overhang on each of the other three sides before attaching. The front extension will be slightly wider than the other two sides. An entrance hole should be cut as shown. Attach the vertical security peice last, if it is to be used.

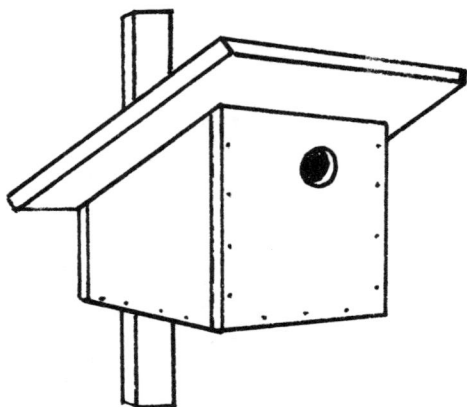

For: wrens, chickadees, titmice, flycatchers, warblers, and other small birds.

HOUSE PLAN NUMBER 17

This little house for small birds is made to be hung from a tree limb or other support. The cylindrical cross-section should be about six inches in diameter and eight inches long. It may be cut from a tree cross-section or a cross-section from a piece of fire wood of adequate diameter. After cutting the cylinder, core the middle to leave a shell of about three-fourths inch thickness. Next, cut one end at 45° slope (⌂), leaving a center peak edge. Cut two roof pieces, one five inches by nine inches (if using one-half inch thick material), or reduced by one-fourth inch on the shorter side, if of plywood. Attach the two pieces together to form the roof, along the nine inch sides. Then nail the roof to the shell cylinder. Cut a bottom piece from a nine inch by nine inch board and attach it to the bottom of the cylinder, with the same extending edges on all sides. The decorative piece around the base of the cylinder may be made of rope or vine. Install a screw eye in the top for hanging the house. The entrance hole should be cut according to the size of the bird that you are planning to attract.

For: chickadees, wrens, titmice, warblers, house finches, and other small birds.

HOUSE PLAN NUMBER 18

This house for small birds is made of two side pieces eight inches by eight inches and a top piece two inches by eight inches. The wedge-shaped ends, two inches (top) by five inches (bottom) by six inches (sides), are cut from the same materials. Assemble by making the back wedge even with the roof edges and by attaching the two side pieces and the top roof piece. Then attach the front wedge about one inch inside the edge of the outside roof frame. This gives a rain protection. The bottom is then cut out, approximately five inches by five inches. Measure for this after assembling the rest of the house. Now cut an entrance hole in the position shown and add a perch if desired. Attach slices of bark to the outside of the house to give it a natural appearance. The completed box may be attached to a post, pole, side of wall, or hung from a limb. Also, it may be set upon a window sill or other favorite place.

For: wrens, chickadees, titmice, warblers, and other small birds.

HOUSE PLAN NUMBER 19

This is a house for small birds, made of an eight inch long half or three-fourths cylinder cross-section of a six-inch diameter limb or tree. Cut one slice three-fourths inches thick from one end of the cylinder. This will be the bottom of the house later. Core the remainder of the cylinder to leave a half-inch or three-fourths inch cylinder shell ( ). Next, cut off about one-fourth of the cylinder ( ). Then cut across one end at an angle to make a sloping top. Be sure that the slope is forward from the back side as shown in the drawing. The top may be cut from a one-fourth inch or one-half inch piece of plywood, cedar, or cypress, eight inches by ten inches. Cut an entrance hole at the position shown in the drawing. Next, use the cylinder cross-section that you have saved as the bottom, cut it to fit the cylinder shell and then attach it to the bottom. You are now ready to attach the house to the back support board. Attach the top with a hinge as shown, leaving a balanced overhang. A perch may be attached by drilling a hole to insert the perch into. Place it immediately below the entrance hole. Use a wood screw to secure the top at the front edge as shown.

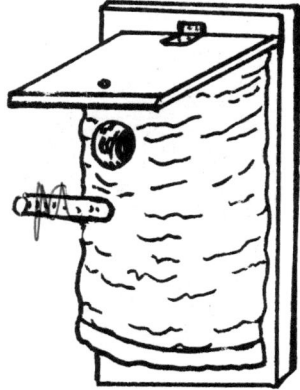

For: nuthatches, wrens, chickadees, titmice, hairy woodpeckers, downy wooodpeckers, and other small birds.

HOUSE PLAN NUMBER 20

This house we are calling a shoebox or mailbox type. It may be square or rectangular in shape, depending upon your preference. If square, perhaps six inches by six inches by six inches will serve. If rectangular, then try six inches by six inches by ten inches. These become the four sides. The ends should be cut out after attaching the sides. Keep the consecutive side attachment scheme () so that the open ends will be square. Then, cut out the ends, approximately four inches by four inches, depending upon the thickness of the material that is being used. We suggest that you measure for this after attaching the sides together. The entrance hole should be cut out of one end piece and about one inch down from the roof piece. Covering the four sides with bark slices or wedges will make an added attraction for the birds. Locate the house in a recommended spot for the particular bird.

For: nuthatches, wrens, titmice, chickadees and other small birds.

HOUSE PLAN NUMBER 21

This decorative house for small birds, especially wrens, is made of a ten-inch long cross-section of log or limb six or eight inches in diameter. Saw two slices about three-fourths inch thick from one end of the cylinder to become the top and bottom of the house. Then saw the cylinder in half vertically (   ), the core to be removed with a chisel, leaving an outer shell about one-half to three-fourths inch thick. Now nail the two half sections together and then attach the top and the bottom. Cut out the entrance hole as shown in the drawing. The upright attachment piece, about two inches by thirty inches, may be cut from cypress, cedar or plywood. Before attaching the end pieces, nail one of the two half-cylinders to the attachment piece, extending above and below. Nail the other half-cylinder to the attached one. Then attach the top and the bottom. The decorative pieces shown are suggestive only.

For: wrens, chickadees, titmice, house finches, and other small birds.

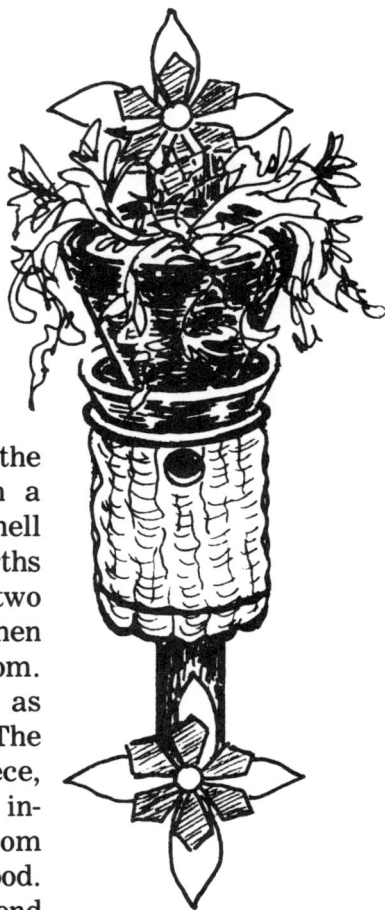

HOUSE PLAN NUMBER 22

This rustic house has varied possibilities of designs. The one shown is covered with small limbs or pieces of cane. Bark slices may also be used, or even live moss attached with a staple gun. The frame is made of your favorite building materials, plywood, cypress, or cedar. The front is four inches by ten inches by five inches and the back is four inches by eight inches. Draw your own irregular pattern for the bottom edge of the front. Cut an entrance hole about one inch from the top of the front side. The perch is made of a two-inch long limb attached horizontally. The two side pieces should be five inches by eight inches and the back should be flush with the sides and roof to permit attaching the house against a tree, wall, or post. An alternative attachment strip, two inches by fourteen inches may be nailed lengthwise for attaching if desired. Assemble the four sides in consecutive order (▣) to make a square. Trace around the framed sides to make a bottom pattern. Cut it out and attach it with nails or hinges for a cleanout. Cut the top end of the framed box to permit a sloping roof pattern as shown. Then attach the roof with overhang in front and flush on the back side. The shown decorative front piece under the roof is optional. The roof may be painted or covered with bark or moss.

For: flickers, small woodpeckers, warblers, titmice, chickadees, and other small birds.

HOUSE PLAN NUMBER 23

This is a typical type of bluebird house that may be attached to a post, pole, or tree, or suspended from a limb for other kinds of birds. The back and front pieces are made six inches by twelve inches, the sides are five and one-half inches by nine inches, and the top pieces, one seven inches by five inches and the other seven inches by five and one-half inches. Attach the two six inch by twelve inch pieces temporarily together and then cut the top angle 45° as shown (⟶). These two boards then become the front and back. Nail the two roof pieces together along the seven inch sides, with the nails through the edge of the seven inch by five inch piece. Now attach the front and back to the two sides. Attach the roof, leaving all of the overhang on the front with an even edge on the back. Cut out the entrance hole as shown. Use the house frame to draw the pattern for the bottom. Cut it out and attach it with hinges for cleaning out regularly. The decorative pieces are of short aluminum tacks that are tacked into the sides. Use your own pattern. Bark may be attached instead, and the length and width may be extended for larger birds.

For: bluebirds, house finches, titmice, chickadees, warblers, small woodpeckers, and other small birds.

HOUSE PLAN NUMBER 24

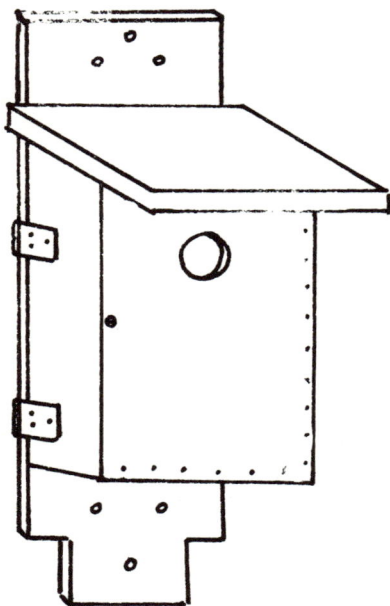

This bluebird house is made of one-fourth or one-half inch thick materials with sides six inches by twelve inches, front six inches by eleven inches, and back six inches by eighteen inches. The top is made seven inches by seven inches. Cut off the two top ends of the side pieces at an angle made by using eleven inches for the front edge and twelve inches for the back edge. Next cut out the bottom piece five and one-half inches, if using one-half inch thick pieces, or five and three-fourths inches by five and three-fourths inches if using one-fourth inch thick pieces. Nail the three sides together as shown in this pattern (⊐), leaving the fourth side to be hinged for the cleanout side. Attach the top with the same amount of overhang on both sides. The left side is now hinged to the back board as shown. A wood screw through the front into the door edge will hold it in place. The bottom edge design of the back board is optional. Use your own pattern for this or make it a straight edge as shown in the drawing. Cut out the entrance hole as shown and attach the house in an appropriate place.

For: bluebirds, house finches, warblers, and other small birds.

HOUSE PLAN NUMBER 25

This house may be hung as a bluebird house by using dimensions of six inches by six inches by twelve inches, or for a smaller bird by using smaller dimensions such as five inches by five inches by six inches. The entrance hole for small birds should be one inch in diameter and for bluebirds it should be one and one-half inches in diameter. Begin your construction by attaching the front and back to the two side pieces so that the sides fit between the front and back flush with their edges. Next, cut a bottom to fit within the bottom opening and nail it into place. Cut the top to fit over the top opening, edges even and not to fit within the opening as was done for the bottom. The perch may be a horizontal one as shown or a perpindicular one if preferred. The top is hinged across the front edge with a brass decorative hinge or hinges as shown. Regular square butt hinges may be used instead. The decorative tack heads are for appearance only and may be of short aluminum tacks, not to protrude on the inside. A bark covering will also lend to the attractiveness of the house.

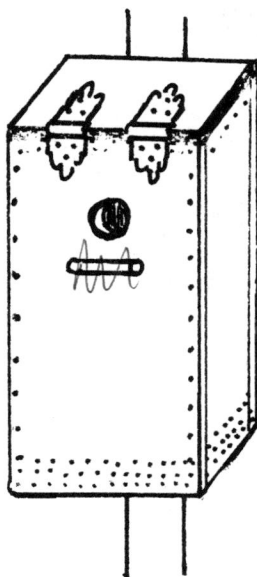

For: small woodpeckers, bluebirds, and other small birds.

HOUSE PLAN NUMBER 26

This house for small birds can be made from your favorite material and covered on the sides with tree bark slabs as shown. This is optional, however. To make the house as shown, cut out a pattern for the front and back that has these dimensions: seven inches across the bottom, 114° angles between bottom and sides, two inch width for sides and two and three-fourths inches for roof ridges. Use a protractor for the angle measurements and a compass to describe the sides ( ). The roof boards are four inches by ten inches. The sides are two inches by eight inches. The bottom is seven inches by ten inches. Attach the sides to the bottom, front, and back. Then, attach roof boards extending over the front. The two top roof forming edges may be planed or sawed at a fitting angle ( ), or they may be left alone with square edges. The entrance hole should be cut about two inches from the peak of the roof.

For: wrens, chickadees, warblers, titmice, small woodpeckers and other small birds.

HOUSE PLAN NUMBER 27

We show this decorative house with living moss attached to the sides (use a staple gun). Don't be surprised, though, if the birds use the moss for nesting material. The perch is made of an appropriate limb of your choice, which also serves to hold the front of the house in place. The screw and washer at the bottom of the front side also serve to hold the front piece securely. Cut two side pieces eight inches by ten inches, front and back six inches by ten inches, bottom and two top pieces six inches by six inches, two sloping roof pieces three inches by nine inches, and one middle roof piece six inches by six inches. Assemble as follows: Attach the sides to the back, flush, and front edges extending beyond front of house about two inches. Nail bottom in place and top in place. Now slope two opposite edges of the remaining six inch by eight inch piece (.) at 45° angle and nail it on the top of the house so that the two sloping edges are over the sides of the house. Then slope a long edge of each of the other roof pieces and attach them to the square sloped roof piece. ( ). Attach the front side. Cut an entrance hole as shown.

For: bluebirds, warblers, titmice, chickadees, house finches, small woodpeckers and other small birds.

HOUSE PLAN NUMBER 28

This house for small birds is similar to house plan number twenty-seven but has a deeper interior. Cut two end pieces, pentagonal in shape (⬠), with these dimensions: base seven inches, 114° angles on sides, sides two inches and roof edges two and three-fourths inches. The roof boards are four inches by fifteen inches, the sides are two inches by fifteen inches and the bottom is seven inches by fifteen inches. Attach the sides to the bottom, front and back, then attach the roof boards extending over the sides. Live moss covering the top will add to the attraction of the house or bark slivers or wedges may be used to cover the exterior of the house as well. The house may be installed on a pole, surface mounted, or suspended from a limb. If surface mounting is used, the back piece should be flush with the sides. A piece of board about two inches by twelve inches by one-half inch may be nailed across the back to mount the house to the side of a tree or post as shown (⚛). The entrance hole should be cut through the front end of the house about an inch from the peak of the front.

For: house finches, titmice, chickadees, warblers, nuthatches, and other small birds.

HOUSE PLAN NUMBER 29

This house is an easily made cylindrical type. It can be varied in length, depending upon the size of the birds that you are striving to attract. Also, the dimensions of the cross-section piece can be varied in diameter for small birds or larger birds, even the woodpecker group. Instead of an end opening, a side opening may be used for woodpeckers with the house turned in a vertical position. The upright kinds may be attached to a tree or post. Cross-sections of dead trees can be used for these houses, provided the shell is of sound condition. Locating the house properly is important as well as is its appearance. Sometimes it is possible to saw out a cylindrical section already with a cavity and entrance hole of former occupant and from a dead tree that has already fallen. This makes an even greater house offering. If such a cross-section is used, it should be attached to the side of an existing dead tree. If placed on the side of a live hardwood, then cover the outside of the house with bark slivers so it will match the tree upon which it is being attached. We suggest making a six inch or eight inch diameter cylinder with a ten or twelve inch length. The ends for the house are made from two slices cut across the cylinder before it is cored.

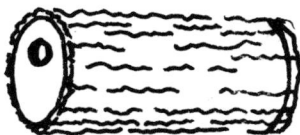

For: wrens, chickadees, titmice, warblers, downy and hairy woodpeckers, nuthatches, and other small birds.

HOUSE PLAN NUMBER 30

This wood duck box is made with a hinged side for cleaning it out each year. The four sides are twelve inches by twenty-four inches, the bottom is eleven and one-half inches, and the top is eighteen inches by eighteen inches. Attach the sides in consecutive order with overlaps (⊡). This makes a square bottom of eleven and one-half inches (if one-half inch thick material is being used). Next, attach the top. Make the back sides even with the edge of the back and with an overhang on the other three sides. The oval shaped entrance can be made by cutting two holes of one inch diameter with three inch centers on a horizontal line that is drawn four inches from the top of the front board edge and six inches from the side edges of the front board. After drilling the two one inch holes, cut a three inch diameter hole by using the midpoints of the horizontal line as the center of your three inch circle, thusly (⊶⊖⊷). Then cut off the four intersection projections that remain between the small circles (see dotted lines). The resulting opening will have a three inch vertical width and a four inch horizontal width. Smooth the edges with a wood rasp or with sand paper.

For: wood ducks.

HOUSE PLAN NUMBER 31

This attractive village hut can be made from a six-inch diameter cross-section log or limb, prepared as described elsewhere but with a straight edge instead of a sloping edge at the top. The roof is made from a semi-circular piece of roofing material, heavy roofing felt, or light sheet metal. Shape the roof as shown by first cutting a circle and then a radius and by folding the radius edges to the desired pitch, bradding them together along the overlap. Use small nails or screws to attach the roof to the house shell. Various decorative roof coverings are possible: pine needles, small cane sections, small limbs, pine cone scales, or other materials of your choice. Attach these before you make the roof cone, while it can be laid flat for attaching. A perch or not is optional. The finished house lends itself to hanging from a limb, setting upon a ledge, or attaching against a wall, tree, or post. It, too, may be varied in size to attract different birds.

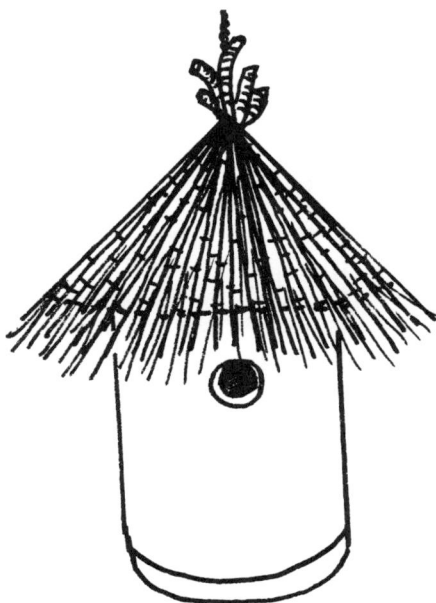

For: wrens, titmice, chickadees, house finches, warblers, small woodpeckers, and other small birds.

HOUSE PLAN NUMBER 32

This wood duck house, made of one inch thick cypress, is similar to plan number thirty-one, except the roof is sloping toward the front slightly and one side opens at the top part only, the other part remaining secured. It is made for monitoring the wood duck nesting procedures particularly. The entrance hole is made like the one described in number thirty-one. In preparing the side that has the door and security piece below it, we suggest that you cut the side piece into the two parts along a 45° slope (Ͷ) to prevent rain from blowing or running inside. These boxes may be installed in a series of three or four together in parallel and a few feet apart, each separate and distinct or they may be installed as singles at various places near the water.

For: wood ducks.

HOUSE PLAN NUMBER 33

This hanging house is an adaptation of house plan number twenty-two, except that the house is placed in the bottom of the macrame piece that you have made for it or bought if you prefer. The flower pot arrangement is held in place at the top by the macrame cords as well as is the base of the house by the bottom cords. The weight of the pot will hold it and the house in a firm position. This can be hung in your favorite patio spot for the wrens or down at the lakeside or wooded area for other species. The macrame motif offers many possibilities as one makes it of heavier or more closely woven materials and by varying the colors to blend properly with the blossoms of the plant and the color of the flower pot. Several of these can be located at different spots around the patio to offer more possibilities of attracting the wrens.

For: wrens and other small birds.

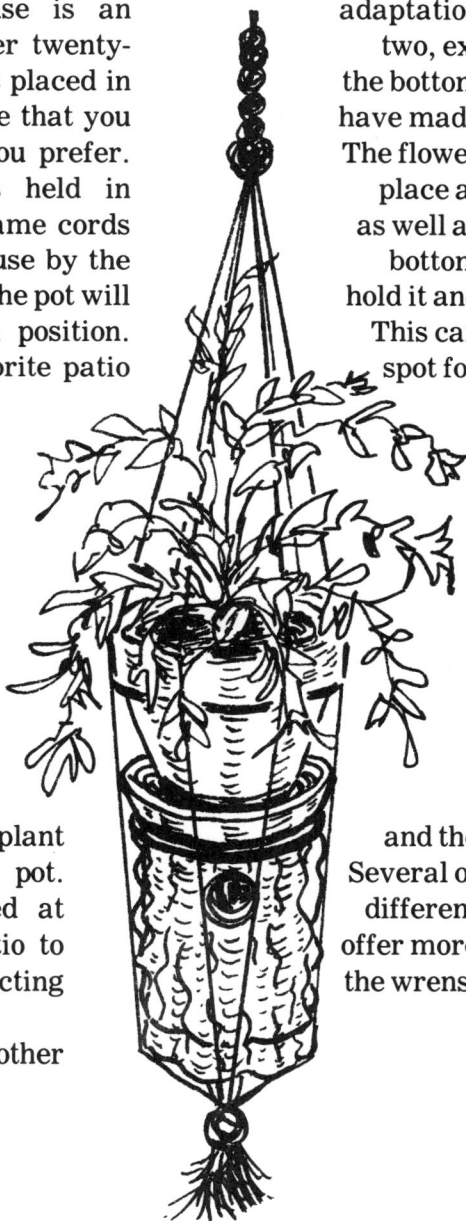

HOUSE PLAN NUMBER 34

This is a bird roosting box for small birds to provide for them a shelter during the cold winter nights. The front piece may be hinged (not shown) to open at the bottom for cleaning or the top may be hinged (shown) for cleaning out the interior. Interior perches are attached, one-fourth inch diameter dowel rods about three inches long, by inserting them through one-fourth inch holes that have been drilled through the sides at selected places. If you put these on both sides of the box interior, it is well to stagger the arrangement on the opposite sides. The entrance hole should not be over two inches in diameter and it should be placed about one inch above the floor level as shown. A perch for entering is shown below the entrance hole. To prevent squirrels from entering the box by cutting the entrance hole larger with their teeth, you may attach a metal ring around the outside of the hole as shown by the dotted line. This may be cut from sheet metal or aluminum. The dimensions for the house pieces are: Back piece twenty-four inches by ten inches, sides eight inches by sixteen inches, from ten inches by fifteen inches, bottom ten inches by eight inches and top ten inches by ten inches.

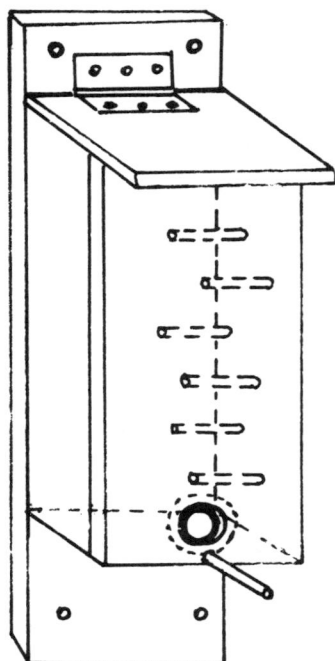

For: all small birds.

HOUSE PLAN NUMBER 35

This house is an adaptation of plan number one. The bottom may be cut to fit inside the cylinder (shown) or for cross-section as shown at the top of the drawing. The back attachment board shows a decorative attachment of your own choosing or this could be omitted. This house also may be modified in size to accommodate the bird of your choice. It can be suspended from a tree limb or other desired location. The entrance hole should be of such size that it will accommodate the bird of your preference.

For: wrens, chickadees, titmice, warblers, violet green swallows, small woodpeckers, and other small birds.

HOUSE PLAN NUMBER 36

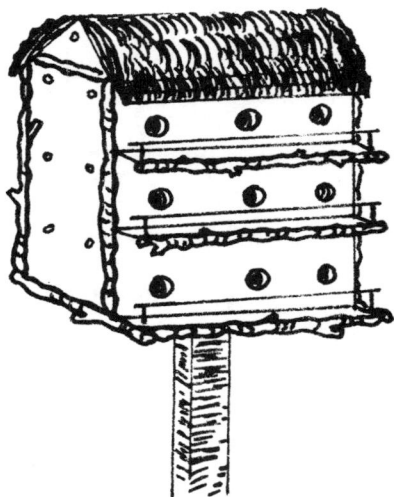

This martin house is a nine-plex with apartments that are eight inches by eight inches, made of your favorite building materials. Cut two pieces eight inches by twenty-four inches (ends), four pieces ten and one half inches by twenty-four inches (floor and ceiling), one piece twenty-four inches by twenty-four inches (back), three pieces seven and two-thirds inches by twenty-four inches (fronts), and two gables described later. These dimensions are for use of one-fourth inch thick plywood. Construct as follows: nail the end pieces to the bottom piece, making the back edges even and extending the front to the floor exterior (porch). Next, eight inches above the floor nail the second floor into place in a similar manner, then the third floor, and then the fourth floor. The fourth floor becomes the ceiling of the third floor. Now nail the back on. Add the partitions eight inches apart. The entrance holes can be cut more easily if done before assembling. Attach the roof to the frame. It will be necessary to spread the roof out a slight bit to make it fit the front and back edges. Loosen the roof nails slightly for this. Now make a pattern for the two roof gables, cut them and nail into place. Dowel rod railings may be installed across the front of the porches as shown. Cover the roof and corners with decorative pieces.

For: purple martins.

HOUSE PLAN NUMBER 37

This twelve-plex martin house may be made of twelve three-pound coffee cans or by using one-fourth inch exterior plywood for partitions and curving sheetmetal for the sides. Cut out three circular pieces of one-fourth inch plywood twenty-two inches in diameter for the floor pieces and the roof. The added sloping metal roof is made of a circular piece of sheetmetal with a twenty-eight inch diameter. After cutting out the circular piece, cut one radius from any position on the circumference. Then by overlapping the two cut edges the degree of pitch for the roof is determined. Brad the two overlapping edges together, from circumference to center. Then arrange the cans six to a floor so that they have the same amount of floor area around the outside of each. They can then be attached by nailing through the thick edges of the cans into the roof (⌁). If using sheetmetal outer covering, cut two rectangular pieces seven inches high and six and one-half feet long. Cut twelve partitions seven inches by eleven inches and nail into place. Lap the sheetmetal into place around the outside and attach with screws or nails. The top is attached to the circular roof piece.

For: purple martins.

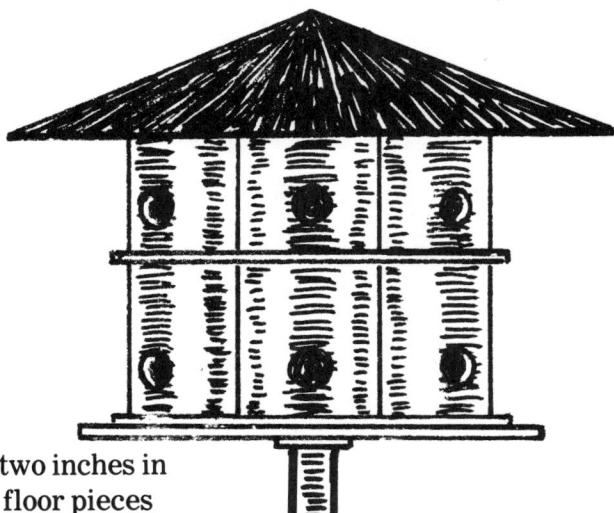

HOUSE PLAN NUMBER 38

This screech owl house is easily made, using the following dimensions: two end pieces eight inches by eight inches with the opposite top corners cut off at 45° angles, two and one-half inches from each top corner; two side pieces eleven inches by five and one half inches, two roof pieces fourteen inches by three inches and a bottom piece eleven inches by nine inches. These measurements are for use of one-half inch thick materials. Make adjustments if one-fourth inch thick material is used. Cut an entrance hole with a two and three-fourth inch diameter, three inches from top edge of front to center of circle and four inches from edges of front to the center of the circle. Begin construction by attaching the eleven inch long sides to the two end pieces, then the three fourteen inch long roof pieces so that the three-inch overhang is on the front side over the entrance hole. Attach the bottom using two butt hinges as shown, with a wood screw on the opposite side to hold the bottom tightly in place. This permits one to clean out the house whenever he desires. Paint the house dark brown, dark gray, leave it to weather, or cover it with bark or bark slabs. Erect it at an appropriate place to attract the screech owl, placed on a horizontal limb or next to the trunk of the tree, from ten to thirty feet high, in a pine, orchard apple or hardwood tree.

For: screech owls and sparrow hawks

HOUSE PLAN NUMBER 39

This barn owl house can be made of one-fourth inch exterior plywood, cypress, or western cedar. If plywood is used, we suggest an exterior covering of bark or bark slabs to give it a more natural appearance. The base piece is ten inches by twenty-eight inches. The top is ten inches by twenty-two inches, and the ends are ten inches by fifteen inches. The two side pieces are twenty-two inches by fifteen inches. One of these side pieces is sawed into two parts, one for a door and one for a lower side piece below the door. The side cleanout door piece is twenty-two inches by ten inches and is hinged with two nails, one at the top edge of each door end. The entrance is square and six inches by six inches. Begin construction by attaching the two end pieces on the two side pieces, the full side and the small twenty-two inch by four inch piece. Now nail the top into place, then the bottom, flush at back end and extending six inches for the porch. Lastly, add the door. It may need to be sanded or planed slightly to permit a loose fitting. A door stop may be added across the two lower inner corners. Also an extended piece installed against the inside middle of the lower piece will permit a screw eye to be used to lock the cleanout door in place as shown.

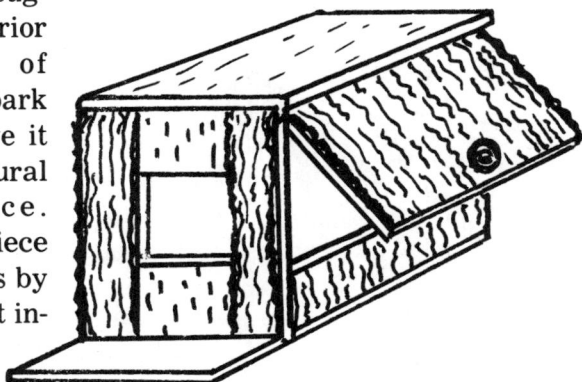

For sparrow hawks, barn owls and other owls.

HOUSE PLAN NUMBER 40

The pigeon house for the pigeon fancier offers several possibilities. He can have a house for a single pair or a colony style house for many. The house shown is for one pair and is located in a dormer of the residence or other house on the premises. It can also be placed up under the eave of any building that has such a projection. To make the house shown you will need to cut the top and bottom twelve inches by eighteen inches, two end pieces twelve inches by ten inches and the front and back pieces ten inches by fifteen inches. The entrance hole should be four inches by six inches with optional curved top (shown) or straight edge (not shown). Begin assembling by nailing the front to the two end pieces and then the back to the two end pieces. Next attach the bottom with an even overhang on the ends and flush with the back. Attach the top the same way. The house can be attached inside the dormer or under the eave at your selected location. If you plan to have a colony of pigeons, then you will need a pigeon loft or pigeon coop and should purchase a book on pigeon raising from your local pet shop for complete instructions.

For: pigeons

SELECTED
BIBLIOGRAPHY

BIBLIOGRAPHY

Bent, Arthur C. **Life Histories of North American Birds** (21 volume set). Washington: Smithsonian Institution Press (United States Natural History Museum) 1919, 1968 (reprinted in paperback by Dover Publications).

This is the most complete study of North American birds that is available, a basic resource set for all naturalists and ornithologists.

Cruickshank, Allen D. and Helen. **1001 Questions Asked About Birds.** Dover reprint of 1958 edition. New York: Dover Publications, 1976.

Sections on migration, breeding, growth, ecology, etc. An excellent quick reference piece for your library.

Darling, Lois and Louise. **Bird.** Boston: Houghton Mifflin, 1962.

A book for bird watchers who wish to go beyond the identification stage. A presentation of scientific writings with clarity and vividness for which the non-specialist will be grateful.

Dorman, Caroline. **Bird Lore.** Baton Rouge, Louisiana: Claitor's Press, Publishing Division, 1969.

A well spun story series by a lifetime birder who learned

the secrets through her intimate terms with the birds on her 120 acre tract of forest, pond, and running streams of Louisiana.

Fisher, James and Roger Peterson. **World of Birds.** New York: Crescent Books, 1964. (New and Revised Edition)

A beautifully illustrated book with 192 full color places. It analyses the biology and way of life of birds with an introduction to ornithology as a science; discusses distribution, dynamics of flight, general anatomy, and the ways a bird lives in the water, air, and forest. It gives suggestions on ways to plan your own bird-watching activities.

Forbush, Edward Howe and John Richard May. **A Natural History of American Birds of Eastern and Central North America.** Boston: Houghton Mifflin, 1939. Reprinted by Bramhall House, New York.

This book, with a well chosen field guide forms a basic library of any ornithologist or naturalist. It is a book for both interest and reference.

Harrison, George H. **Roger Tory Petersons Dozen Birding Hotspots.** New York: Simon and Schuster, 1976.
Describes in detail the twelve best places in North America for seeing the most spectacular array of birds and bird behavior. The text is supplemented by beautiful photographs and a special section follows each chapter with tips on what to take; where to stay; how far ahead to plan and where to write for information; availability of groceries, gas, campsites, and restaurants.

Hines, Bob and Peter A. Anastasi. **Fifty Birds of Town and City**. Washington: United States Department of the Interior, 1973.

A concise, one-page description with illustration in color. A quick, ready reference for a most concise summary.

Immhoff, Thomas. **Alabama Birds**. Second Edition. University of Alabama: University of Alabama Press, 1976.

Describes 378 species found in Alabama, 365 birds in color. Serves for other southern states as well and most birds for every state. A very complete treatise.

Krutch, Joseph Wood and Paul S. Eriksson. **A Treasury of Bird Lore**. New York: Paul S. Eriksson, Inc. 1962.

A rich compilation of writings for every taste, written by almost every significant naturalist since Mark Catesby. There are five parts: Flight (13 authors), Family Matters (14 authors), Birds of a Feather (24 authors), Birds and Men (24 authors), Extinction and Conservation (9 authors). This is your chance to have narrative stories by over 80 favorites.

Laycock, George. **The Birdwatcher's Bible**. New York: Doubleday and Company, Inc., 1976.

Contains information on attracting birds to your feeding stations, how to find and identify birds, bird photography, and song recordings, bird watching sites in the different states, with 205 photos.

Layton, Reber B. **The Purple Martin**. Jackson, Miss.:
Nature Books Publishers, 1969

This is the only book on the species that is endorsed by
national and international ornithologists. It is a complete and authentic guide to one of America's favorite
birds. Well illustrated with photographs and drawings.

Lowery, H. George, Jr. **Louisiana Birds**. Third Edition.
Baton Rouge, Louisiana: Louisiana Wildlife and
Fisheries Commission, by L.S.U. Press, 1974.

Describes 411 species of birds that have been observed
in Louisiana; generously illustrated, with a discussion
on each bird. Serves for other southern states as well
and most birds for any state. This is a very complete
treatise of the bird life of the 411 birds.

Parker, Bertha Morris. **Baby Birds**. Racine, Wisconsin:
Golden Press. 1964.

This is a 25 page paperback activity book of Natural
Science, well done and quite entertaining for the "wee"
one, the early beginning birder.

Peterson, Roger Tory. **A Field Guide to the Western Birds**.
(Second Edition). Boston: Houghton Mifflin, 1961.

This is a companion piece for the birds of the west and
includes Hawaii.

_____, **A field Guide to the Birds**. (Second Edition).
Boston: Houghton Mifflin, 1947.

This is one of the standard guides for identifying birds east of the Rockies.

Pettingill, Olin Sewall, Jr. **A Guide to Bird Finding East of the Mississippi.** Second Edition. New York: Oxford Press, 1977.

Covers 26 eastern states, 725 pages and 85 drawings. Updated after 25 years, it takes into account changes in the environment, noting where habitats have disappeared and where others have remained publicly owned and secure.

Pettit, Ted. **Birds of Your Back Yard.** New York: Avenel Books, 1949.

This little book gives an interesting narrative of ways to attract birds, identify, feed, and house them.

Potzger, J.E. and Gladys M. Friesner. **Birds to Know.** Buffalo, New York: Kenworthy Educational Services, 1968.

For the young birders, a factual book to serve as a background for an understanding of bird study and bird life and to develop appreciation and sympathy for birds. It covers 45 common birds of the United States. Each lesson is accompanied by authentic, simple line drawings with directions to color, offering interesting and constructive activity for the young birders.

Pough, Richard H. **Audubon Land Bird Guide.** New York: Doubleday and Company, 1946.

All 275 species in full color illustration. Excellent field guide.

Reilly, Edgar M. Jr. **The Audubon Illustrated Handbook of American Birds.** New York: McGraw Hill, 1968.

While not a handbook to be carried about in the pocket, it is a comprehensive, informative, thorough, definitive description of the habits, life history, and appearances of every bird in the United States — nearly 875 species. It is "the book to which we turn when we want some item of information about a species or group of species, stated precisely, with brevity, and, above all, authority", notes Dr. Olin Sewell Pettingill, Jr., the editor in chief, in his foreward.

Robbins, Chandler S., Bertle Bruun and Herbert Zim. **Birds of North America.** New York: Golden Press, 1966.

A concise one volume book for all North American birds. A favority field guide among birders. Information readily available. The author's recommendation for the most useful of field guides.

Wetmore, Alexander, et al. **Song and Garden Birds of North America.** Washington: National Geographic Society, 1964.

This covers 327 species in color and fully described. A rich compilation of writings by imminent ornithologists. Beautifully done.

Zeleny, Laurence. **The Bluebird.** Bloomington, Indiana:

Indiana University Press, 1976.

A summary of the scientific literature about this species and over 50 years of personal experience by the author, well known for his promotion of bluebirds across America.

Zim, Herbert S. and Ira N. Gabrielson. **Birds: A Guide to the Most Familiar American Birds** (A Golden Guidebook). New York: Simon Schuster, 1949.

A long time standard, easily used pocket guide for the beginner and the more knowledgeable. Information at your fingertips.

APPENDIX

BIRD HOUSE AND
BIRD FEEDER RETAILERS

Listed below are three long established commercial houses from which bird houses and feeders may be purchased, if you prefer not to build your own. A catalogue is available from each for the asking.

Audubon Workshop, 1501 Paddock Drive, Northbrook, Illinois 60062

Hyde Bird Feeders, Hyde's of Waltham, 56 Felton Street, Waltham, Massachusetts 02154

Duncraft, Wild Bird Specialists, 25 South Main Street, Penacook, New Hampshire 03301.

There are a number of other good supply houses also.

ORNITHOLOGICAL SOCIETIES

For the birder who desires to keep up with current happenings in the avian world he will find one or all of the following important ornithological societies helpful.

American Ornithological Union

membership -	open
publication -	**The Auk,** free to members
address -	Secretary, Dr. George E. Watson, National Museum of Natural History, Smithsonian Institution Washington, D.C. 20560
dues -	$8.00 annually

Cooper Ornithological Society

membership -	open
publication -	**The Condor,** free to members
address -	Jane R. Durham, Oakland Museum, 1000 Ash Street, Oakland, California 90024
dues -	$12.00 annually

Wilson Ornithological Union

membership -	open
publication -	**The Wilson Bulletin** - free to members
address -	Dr. Jerome Jackson, Department of Zoology, Mississippi State University, Mississippi State University, Mississippi State University, Mississippi 39762
dues -	$8.00 annually

National Audubon Society

membership -	open
publication -	**Audubon Magazine** and **American Birds,** mag. free to members
address -	National Audubon Society, 950 Third Avenue, New York, N.Y. 10022
dues -	$15 annually
	$18 family

There are many splendid state and local organizations that carry on extensive work in the field of birding and ornithology. These are too numerous to mention, but each will offer aid to the interested birder. Check with your local chamber of commerce or the state chamber of commerce.

INDEX